CONNECT & ENJOY MORE CONTENT

Engaging with readers is one of the most rewarding aspects of my writer's journey. Stay in touch
(and get exclusive content) by subscribing to my
mailing-list for the *Smokeless Mirror*, a place
where faith, history, adventure, and self-discovery
intersect.

– Shawn

SMOKELESSMIRROR.COM/SUBSCRIBE

A THOUSAND MILES TO SANTIAGO

MOMENTS AND MEDITATIONS ALONG EUROPE'S GREAT PILGRIMAGE

SHAWN HERRON

Smokeless Mirror L.L.C.

First edition

Date of publication: November 2022

ISBN-13: 979-8-9857799-0-5 (hardcover)
ISBN-13: 979-8-9857799-1-2 (ebook)

Published by Smokeless Mirror L.L.C.
SMOKELESSMIRROR.COM

Editor: Elayne Morgan
SERENITYEDITINGSERVICES.COM

Cover Design: Andy Bridge
ANDYBRIDGE.COM

Book Interior: Colleen Sheehan
AMPERSANDBOOKERY.COM

Maps: Nat Case, INCase, LLC
INCASELLC.COM/NAT

Cover design inspired by the artwork of Arthur Hawkins, Jr. (1903-1985) from his book design for *The Postman Always Rings Twice* [Alfred A. Knopf Inc., 1934], written by James M. Cain (1892-1977).

Pilgrims depicted on the back of book were inspired from a sculpture by Vicente Galbete that stands on top of Alto de Perdon (Hill of Forgiveness) along the Camino Francés (after Pamplona, Spain).

To my parents, Patrick and Mary Herron. Your love and support have made all the difference in my life.

TABLE OF
CONTENTS

"Audentis Fortuna Iuvat"

(Fortune Favors the Bold)

VIRGIL'S "AENEID"

FRANCE

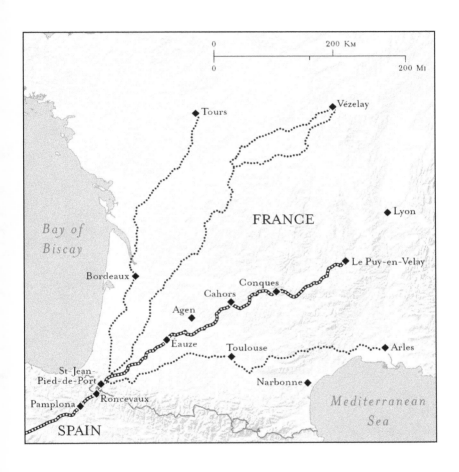

The Calling

In the dim confines of a fifth century cathedral, I peer around the solemn space, seeking an exit. There's a staircase at the center of the floorplan and I notice a natural light coming up the stairs, so I head over.

Figuring the steps will lead me outside, I adjust the hefty pack on my shoulders and follow the light. At the bottom of the steps, I reach a space resembling a cavern. A high archway up ahead frames today's cloudy morning sky, and I approach it.

Standing underneath the archway, I can see a valley down below. My thoughts begin to wander as I look out toward the green hills just beyond the sea of red terracotta roofs within the low grounds.

What a difference a year makes. Twelve months ago, I was ending my career in Washington, DC, and saying farewell to friends and coworkers. Today, I'm standing outside an ancient cathedral just above another series of steps leading to a remote town in central France.

Built around a volcanic hill, this ancient town wraps itself around the mount's entirety, and a maze of narrow streets weaves its way from the base up and around to its pinnacle, where the cathedral behind me sits like a crown.

Welcome to Le Puy-en-Velay, a town situated on the southeastern edge of France's Auvergne region. This region is known for striking landscapes of huge volcanic rock masses jutting out from its valley floors, just like the hill I'm standing on now.

I refocus my sight from the distant treeline to the succession of steps just below my feet. My eyes follow their descent all the way to the stone-lined street below, with stone-slab buildings on both its left and right as it travels down the hill. Along the street's center is a black rock path interrupting the otherwise silver tone of the town. This path represents the beginning of my latest journey, an ancient pilgrimage known as *The Way*. In France, it's called *Le Chemin*, but most people know it by its Spanish name—*El Camino*.

Coming from Aix en Provence, I had meant to start my journey here yesterday. However, after some confusion with the French attendant at one of my transfer points—followed by my subsequent ride aboard the wrong train for the next several hours—my start date had to be put on hold for a day.

Language Barrier = 1   Me = 0

So here I am on a mid-September morning, a day later than expected, about to begin a near-thousand-mile walk toward the western reaches of Spain, to the city of Santiago de Compostela.

What awaits me out there? I'm not exactly sure. That's what I'm here to find out.

I readjust the large pack on my shoulders, noticing its substantial weight. Ugh. I take a deep inhale and begin descending the stairs, taking my first few steps as a pilgrim. Moving into the street's corridor, I pass a succession of old yet pristinely kept houses. At this early hour, Le Puy has yet to stir. The pilgrims I met at this morning's mass have already left. The few folks I do see are unloading a truck full of decorations for a festival taking place here this coming weekend.

Already in place are wooden poles standing at regular intervals down both sides of the street. Each has a medieval crest affixed near the top, while long streams of yellow and blue linen have been strung from the top of one pole to the next down both sides of the street as far as the eyes can see. It's as if the town is being staged for a royal visit.

The townspeople are actually preparing Le Puy for a yearly Renaissance festival, when the town is transformed back into its former glory.

Thousands from the region come dressed in medieval attire, ready to reenact the daily rituals of their ancestors. This adds an unexpected twist of irony as I step out on foot, just like a pilgrim would have done a millennium ago. It's as if the past is giving me a wink and welcoming me back into the fold.

Next I pass by some local shops: a few cafés, a boulangerie, an antique bookshop. Perhaps little has changed here in recent years, but this region used to be part of Gaul. This town's history actually stretches back some five thousand years, well before the ascendant Julius Caesar and the Romans took control of Gaul (modern-day France) by defeating the Celts back in 52 BC.[1] While the Polytheistic Romans incorporated the Gaulish territories into their empire,[2] by the third century, Le Puy had earned a special spiritual significance for early Christians. The pinnacle I just left is the site of the first recorded Marian Apparition.

In the third century, a woman suffering from an incurable illness came to the top of the vol-

canic mount to pray for her life. Already present
was a large megalithic black stone, part of an
ancient dolmen—a sort of tomb made up of a
few stones—which had been incorporated into
a pagan altar.[3] As the woman lay beside this
ancient dolmen, Mother Mary is said to have
appeared to her atop it, and through Mary's intercession, the woman's illness was miraculously
cured. Mary then requested the site be built up
as a sanctuary to her, which led to a cathedral
eventually being built on that very spot, with the
powerful dolmen placed within.[4]

Word of this 'Stone of Visions' spread, and
when other reported miracles followed, a Great
Marian Pilgrimage was born. Saints, popes,
kings, queens, and even emperors would one
day make pilgrimage here to venerate the Virgin
Queen. Throughout the Middle Ages, Le Puy
grew in size as well as influence, becoming one
of Mary's holiest shrines in all of Europe. A
portion of the dolmen can still be found inside its
walls, along with a mysterious Black Madonna of
unknown origin, likely from the Jewish Levante.[5]

Le Puy, though, is my starting point, and right now I'm finding my way down its twisting streets, looking for the little red and white markers that are posted at each turn to guide pilgrims out of the city and in the direction of Santiago de Compostela. Before leaving entirely, I take a quick detour, veering off to my right to get a glimpse of the two other sacred sites within the valley.

The closer and taller of these sites is a huge rock face beside the mount I just walked down. The volcanic pedestal reaches high above the cathedral I was in. On top of the huge pedestal stands *La Statue de Notre Dame de France*, a fifty-foot-tall bronze statue of Mary overlooking the town. She holds a young Jesus, whose hand is reaching out to the world to bless it.

The other sacred site, a little further off in the distance, is a steep volcanic spire. Its craggy exterior shoots straight up to the peak, where a chapel is perched on top, looking as if it has grown directly out of this volcanic mass.

This elevated chapel, Saint-Michel d'Aiguilhe, is dedicated to Archangel Michael. A bishop named Godescalc is said to have constructed the chapel; interestingly enough, he is also credited as the first recorded foreigner to make the long pilgrimage to Santiago de Compostela. Living back in the tenth century, Bishop Godescalc traveled to Santiago to visit the shrine of Saint James the Greater, an apostle whose remains were said to have been discovered there a century prior, after having been lost for nearly eight hundred years.

The bishop's pilgrimage established a link between these two sanctuaries. The 'Le Puy route' became known as the *Via Podiensis*, and it turned into one of France's four sacred routes leading to Santiago. This route guides pilgrims nearly five hundred miles to the Pyrenees mountains, followed by another five hundred miles across northern Spain to Santiago de Compostela, where hundreds of thousands of pilgrims began to visit Saint James's shrine each year after Godescalc's own journey.

I'm not sure what compelled the bishop to embark on such a long journey all those years ago. All I know is that I'm attempting to be the latest.

My own interest in this pilgrimage was sparked by a series of coincidences. A little over a year ago, I had never even heard of the Camino, but just as I was resigning from my job and planning a year of travel, it was brought to my attention on three separate occasions, all within a single week.

While these signs were subtle, I couldn't ignore their timing. Call it my gut, call it intuition, but I felt that *something* was calling me to this ancient pilgrimage. I just couldn't be sure as to why. All I could do was trust that these signs were, in fact, leading me to something, and hope that by the end, I'd have figured out what that 'something' could be.

Walking a thousand miles based on a feeling— some would call this bold; others, reckless. But I've found that when the universe is trying to tell you something, it's best to listen.

From what I've gathered, a pilgrimage seems to be an ancient rite of passage. But what purpose could one still serve today? This world no longer resembles the medieval one in which the Camino reached its greatest prominence. For some reason, though, this pilgrimage has been experiencing a resurgence as of late. I don't personally know anyone who's walked it, but from the few second-hand accounts I have heard, a common theme emerged—the person's life had been forever changed by the experience. With my curiosity piqued, I added the Camino to the end of my year-long trip (my first stops were in Nepal, Sri Lanka, and the Seychelles).

Today the Via Podiensis travels along the GR-65, a long-distance walking trail that begins near Geneva, Switzerland. It travels west across all of France, and once passing Le Puy, it goes through the same historic towns pilgrims would have walked through on their way to Spain centuries ago.

Reaching the outskirts of Le Puy, my fellow pilgrims and I walk by farmlands with fields rolling out to green hills that stretch along the background. We follow the path along country roads, passing one farm after another, keeping a lookout for the next turn to take. Each turn along the Via Podiensis is marked by a set of dashes, a white one above a red. They're painted onto anything that presents itself at that moment—be it the side of a building, a fence post, or a rock.

For the next several hours, our route cuts through an endless array of farms. Here in the Haute-Loire part of France, we pass by many small settlements with only a few structures. Fortunately, each of these hamlets has a sign posting the name of the neighboring settlement and its estimated distance. They're all listed in kilometers, though, forcing me to adjust my American sense of distance away from our beloved miles (10 km ≈ 6.2 mi).

As my day progresses, I become accustomed to following markers and approximating distances. What I *haven't* gotten used to is the weight of my pack, which feels like it's getting heavier with each passing hour. Though I'm in decent shape and have done some training leading up to this walk, this is really the first time I'm feeling the true weight of all my belongings.

This is only Day 1—and I haven't even encountered any daunting hills yet—but it's already obvious that if I'm going to make it all the way to Santiago, I have some important decisions to make about what to carry. Deciding to keep my first day short, I find communal lodging in a small village named Montbonnet just sixteen kilometers from Le Puy.

On Day 2, the Camino moves along green rolling fields, then drops down into dense forests and undisturbed meadows. Our route then travels back up along a high ridge plateau, and we walk by a gorgeous array of hills and valleys.

Moving away from Le Puy, we travel deeper and deeper into the countryside, and further and further from traditional life. I've met a decent number of pilgrims already, but my walk has been spent mostly in solitude. The journey continues to be an interesting blend of nature and architecture, taking me past rundown mills and abandoned chateaus. Wayside crosses are posted at the edge of many of these properties, proudly proclaiming this to be God's country.

Unfortunately, my thoughts can't seem to rise above my shoulders due to the weight of my pack. By the end of Day 2, I find a post office, where I send the box of items I've deemed expendable back to the States. Goodbye, notebooks. So long, wireless keyboard.

If I was expecting relief on the following day, I didn't find any. Beginning at the bottom of a wooded gorge, the Camino zigzags up the far side of a massive ravine. The route climbs for hours along dirt tracks weaving up to the high woodlands. It feels like my shoulders are carrying a house instead of an overloaded backpack; the steepness of the gorge only exacerbates this point. Our climb keeps rising and rising—so much so that, by the end of Day 3, I'm back at another post office, ready to shed whatever else

I can, my definition of 'expendable' expanding
with each passing day.

With a limited budget and a looming winter,
I can't just discard everything in my pack. I have
to account for multiple seasons if I'm going to
endure the elements. I have to think about everything in my pack differently, though. "Ounces
equal pounds," goes the old military adage. To
make it through this ordeal, I must identify what
is important and discard any excess.

Outside the post office, I pull each item from
my pack and scrutinize everything: lights, bat-
teries, food, socks, soaps, tops, bottoms, towels,
canisters, even coins. I strip away all I can spare,
leaving myself with little more than a few changes
of clothes, a sleeping bag, and some cold weather
gear to sustain me for the next couple of months.

After this second postal drop, I finally do find
some relief, allowing me to focus on some of the
more pleasant aspects of my journey. As the days
roll on, late summer soon becomes early fall, the
perfect time of year for walking. This is when
the autumn breeze cools the skin, and a gentle

sun warms it up. The colors of the leaves change, as do the landscapes region to region. Our Camino travels alongside stone-wall framed pastures of the Lozèr, then over the cattle-grazed hills of the Aveyron. I become accustomed to seeing more cows than people each day, a far cry from normal life back in the States.

This whole year of travel has actually been about letting go of what was 'normal', about seeing the world without the restraints of a job, embracing the unknown, and allowing life to lead me where it may. By the age of thirty-five, I've come to know many roles in life. To my family, I'm a son, a brother, an uncle, and now a godfather. In school, I was a student and an athlete. After college, I was a soldier, a government contractor, and then a government employee. I was raised Catholic, and though I was born in the United States, I grew up knowing my Irish heritage well.

By this point in life, I'm familiar with both success and failure. I've known my fair share of joys and sorrows. I've measured up to certain moments, and have faltered in others. From what I've come to know regarding success, it rarely comes easily. Anything worth doing requires effort; typically, the greater the challenge, the greater the reward.

It takes preparation and discipline to achieve something. There's no one way to accomplish anything, but in pursuit of a goal, the ability to think, to adapt, to endure are all valuable attributes, and they can take a person far. Other people may find a person's goal unrealistic or unattainable, but dreamers will dream nonetheless. If someone believes they can accomplish a feat, they may feel compelled to go after it despite any naysaying. Each endeavor will be unique, so it's always up to the dreamer to find a way there.

So far, the life of a pilgrim seems to be uncomplicated, and routines have formed quickly. After breakfast each morning, we pack our bags and go, walking as far as our legs will take us. Daily decisions are limited. Can I find lunch along the way or must I buy something beforehand and carry it with me? How many kilometers shall I walk today: twenty, thirty, forty? Umm... No, no; thirty will do.

Depending upon the day, I'll walk alone or with a few other pilgrims. Typically I see fifteen to twenty pilgrims on any given day. This is a low number, I'm told, compared to the summer months.

While walking from place to place, I'll meet pilgrims in almost every town along the route. Some I'll meet while taking a break on the side of the road; others I may see in the fields enjoying a quiet picnic lunch, and I simply give them a wave as I pass by.

Many locals speak only French, though I've found a decent number of English-speaking pilgrims to share conversation with. The pilgrims I've met are from all walks of life. One day I'll be walking with an Austrian farmer, another day it'll be a French chef, an Irish musician, or a Hungarian teacher.

Each night, we'll stay in a *gîte*, a cross between a bed-and-breakfast and a dormitory. When I arrive and ask the gîte managers in French if they have an available bed for the night, all I hope to hear is a clear *Oui* or *Non*. If I don't, and they just start stringing sentences together, then I'll surely be lost and have to repeat my original question once again: *"Umm, avez-vous un lit ce soir?"*

Once I settle in, I'll mingle with other pilgrims. A group of us will usually go exploring the place we're calling home for the evening, which could be a village hidden deep within a wooded valley, such as Saint-Chély d'Aubrac, or a town nestled along a restful river, like Espalion.

Some of these gîtes are rather nice. Give me a hot shower and a clean bed and I'm content, but I'll never tire of waking up, walking into the dining area, and finding the table stacked with warm baguettes fresh from the boulangerie, accompanied by whipped butter and homemade jams—fig, apricot, and chocolate with orange— to smear over top.

Most of our stays along the Camino have been pleasant. As to the more basic, less cozy gîtes—well, you'll just be happy to be leaving in the morning. Still, being comfortable with discomfort is all part of the adventure, because the pilgrim life, though simple, is not easy.

The Camino's reputation as being 'unforgiving' is justified. Walking such long distances, with your pack weighing down your shoulders day after day, grinds your body down until your legs ache and your feet blister; then your steps feel like daggers are being thrust through your boots, piercing your feet and sending razor-blade-ridden lightning bolts up your legs and body.

Agony. It's spared no one, and never have I met a pilgrim with enough time to simply stop and let their body fully heal. An occasional rest day is all anyone can afford, so that leaves two options—keep walking or stop completely.

When your body is tired and in pain, the mind becomes the biggest hurdle. You no longer notice the cool autumn breeze, nor do you care about that gentle warm sun. You may even start to wonder if someone secretly added weight to your pack while you weren't looking, a cruel joke that no one but your own mind, or maybe an old Army buddy, would play. And if you're a spiritual person—which not everyone who walks the Camino today is—you'll be praying for God's mercy. Hopefully you'll get it.

Each of us works to find a rhythm as we deal with our individual pain. As we become accustomed to the pilgrim lifestyle, it offers us a new perspective, one of shared suffering, bringing us together in our journey. Starting from the limited view of our individual lives, our physical pains help us to relate to one another, expanding our outlook to consider more than just ourselves. This shift seems important because, while we all have our own personal experiences, our time on earth will always remain a shared existence.

Moving forward, history opens up to us through the Camino. As we follow the footsteps of pilgrims who've walked before us, the past reveals itself through the places we experience along the way, many of them well over a thousand years old.

Continuing along, stories of ancient pilgrims echo from the dust beneath our feet. Shuffling forward, we stir up their memory, bringing them new life. Out here we're able to look back and see how they lived, and what they valued, in a way a classroom never can never simulate.

As we'll come to see, the Camino isn't just *connected* to history—it has become one with it, and its stories reveal themselves as our journey unfolds.

Her Majesty

[The Spirit of Sainte Foy]

About a third of the way through France, a few pilgrims and I approach a village hidden deep within the wilderness. As we descend through the forest and look down the hillside, we first see the village as an assemblage of steep slate roofs. Continuing downward, the village's stone and half-timbered façades begin to reveal themselves. Upon reaching it, the view opens up below us to show groupings of medieval houses clustered within a small valley resembling a shell.

We've arrived at the majestic village of Conques—the first major milestone on the Via

Podiensis—a refuge of stone set along a gorge within the secluded hills of northern Aveyron. Below us is the rear side of a magnificent abbey church made with a blend of yellow limestone, pink sandstone, and gray-blue schist. As we emerge from the woods, the church's steeple and twin bell towers are high up near our eye level, and its oval apse is visible a few stories below.

Leading down to the village, a cobbled street half-spirals around the right side of the church and down toward the front, allowing us a close-up look at the large structure and the unconventional panes in its arched windows, which span the church's three stories.

Almost absent of color, these windows have been fitted with alternating strips of glazed translucent glass in varying shades of gray. They are a more recent addition to this church by Pierre Soulages, the French artist who created them specifically for this structure, the very site that inspired him to become an artist.[6]

The cobbled street brings us down to the village center, and we enter a plaza in front of the church. Its twin bell towers are high above us now. Between the two is a tall stone façade. It has a simple design except for the space above the main entrance, where a tympanum is carved into the stone above a set of double wooden doors, with graphic images telling the story of the Last Judgment.[7]

Such a large church for such a tiny village. But this little place has a grand story—one involving the small, mischievous Sainte Foy, whose spirit is known for performing unusual miracles as well as playful pranks on her faithful followers.

Walking around the right side of the church, we come to a huge stone building which will serve as our quarters for the night. This building is part of a retired Benedictine monastery where, for a millennium, hundreds of monks called this place home each year as they worked to perfect themselves while venerating the glorious Sainte Foy, whose relics remain here today.

Foy's story didn't begin in Conques, which only came into existence centuries later. Instead, Foy's life began in a place called Agen, a prosperous city a hundred miles west of here, situated along a major Roman road connecting Rome to Bordeaux.[8]

Sainte Foy (pronounced *Fwah*) was born at the end of the third century, well after the inhabitants of Gaul had become a Roman province. A million Gallic people had died fighting in that conflict, and another million were enslaved, in the process of becoming "civilized" in the eyes of Rome.

During Foy's life, Rome was coming into its eleventh century of existence, one less than the 'prophecy of the twelve eagles' is said to have revealed to Romulus, its founder. Twelve is the mystical number representing the lifetime of Rome, with each eagle representing one century.[9]

At this time, the Roman Empire was still at the apex of its power. While the empire was no stranger to conflict, especially along its borderlands, Christianity was influencing the empire from within, including here in Gaul, where this spiritual movement was on the rise.

REMEMBRANCE

The Roman Empire had always been a pagan society; yet while the Romans welcomed many foreign gods into their pantheon, the Christian movement proved unique. The Jewish faith had its own Messianic prophecy, one which heralded the coming of a suffering servant, a redeemer of mankind, one who would show them the way to God and who would die at the hands of his own people.[10]

Back in the eighth century of Rome's existence, a man named Jesus appeared in Judea preaching love, brotherhood, and forgiveness. Witnesses said he also performed many miracles.

In Jesus's time, Jewish society saw the Creator as more of a wrathful God, ruling by fear and demanding sacrifices in His name. Jesus spoke out against such practices—including punishments promoted by the Pharisees, such as public stonings—claiming that condemning others would just lead to one's own condemnation.

Many Jews who witnessed these miracles and listened to his teachings came to think of him as the prophesied Messiah. They hoped he would free them from Roman oppression as Moses had done with the Egyptians; however, Jesus spoke not of worldly power, but of a hidden kingdom and a path to everlasting life.

Jesus declared he had not come to destroy man, but to save him. He said force was not the way, and he chose not to take on the Romans directly. His words were, rather, those of a reformer, challenging the ways of his own people.

He warned his listeners that if they wanted to enter God's kingdom, their deeds would have to be much more righteous than those of the Pharisees, who posed as holy men through public spectacle and outward ritual and dress, but were only really interested in stroking their own vanity. While they did very little to ease the suffering of those around them, they never missed a chance to praise each other for their piety.

Jesus saw a world made not in the image of God, but in the image of man. He claimed his people had lost their way and were being led astray by shepherds seeking adoration from their fellow man instead of the approval of the Father; moving themselves away from God, rather than toward Him.

Jesus called on listeners to repent and come back to God. Anyone seeking redemption had to turn from wickedness and transform their lives so they could receive Him. Jesus spoke of the Father as a gentle God. He still talked of His love for lawfulness, justice, and righteousness, but he also proclaimed that God is Love. God is Mercy. For those perceiving God as jealous or vengeful, this new understanding of him seemed foreign, but Jesus taught that *God* was not punishing man. Rather, man punishes *himself* by cutting himself off from God.

As it began with John the Baptist, the penitent among Jesus' listeners were given a baptism of repentance for the remission of sins. Once they had confessed their misdeeds, Jesus' disciples dipped them into water to wash away their sins to signify their spiritual rebirth.

Jesus told listeners that God would know them by their good deeds,[11] and that anyone who does the will of God is family.[12] By becoming pure of heart, they would come to know that God is everywhere and in everything. By keeping God's divine precepts, they'd increase in knowledge as well as wisdom, and makes progress toward becoming more like God. They'd begin to love as He loves, "for love is of God; and everyone who loves is born of God and knows God. He who does not love does not know God, for God is love."[13]

Jesus shared his message in the temples, within the synagogues, along the countryside, and around the mountains, and thousands came to hear his precepts on holy living. While Moses had brought the Jewish people the Law, Jesus said he came to arm them with Truth. He even elaborated on Moses' Ten Commandments. First and foremost, he told listeners, they must love God with all their heart, all their soul, and all their mind. Second, they must love their neighbor as if they were themselves. These, he said, were the two most important commandments, and they laid the foundation for all the others.[14] Then he pushed the concept even further, beyond loving their neighbors; Jesus told everyone to love their enemies as well.

While his ideas seemed unique, Jesus' deeds were said to be otherworldly. He was said to cure every ailment. All who visited him seeking God's mercy were healed: The blind would see, the deaf would hear, the lame would walk, and the lepers would be cleansed.[15] Even his disciples were left awestruck, wondering what manner of man this was who could do such wonders as these,[16] though Jesus claimed he could do nothing without the Father Almighty.

His followers considered him the Word—God's Divine Wisdom, incarnate on earth.[17] While his followers thought him to be the Messiah, Jerusalem's High priests were fearful of Jesus and reasoned his miracles were the work of Satan, who wanted to destroy their religion. Jesus told them he did not come to tear down their prophets, but to fulfill their prophesies.[18] Still, the High

Priests decided to conspire against him. After a three-year ministry, Jesus was arrested by Jewish authorities, convicted of blasphemy, and turned over to the Romans, who sentenced him to death.

After the Romans crucified Jesus in Jerusalem, his disciples, whom Jesus called apostles, said that their teacher appeared to them again and told them to spread his message of redemption throughout the known world. Traveling along the Roman roads, the apostles began evangelizing across the empire and beyond.

Jesus Christ's disciples proclaimed him to be the Savior, but Jewish leaders still deemed his teachings to be a threat, a cancer that needed to be excised, and a chasm grew between the two sides. In Antioch, followers of this new way were derogatorily referred to as "christianos"—meaning "little Christs" in Greek—and the name stuck.

Nearly all the apostles were put to death. Yet by the end of their lifetimes, the seeds they planted across the empire had begun bearing fruit. After decades of evangelizing to both Jews and Gentiles, Christian worship was now taking place in small pockets within many of the Roman provinces.

Jesus' original disciples still saw themselves as Jews. While they believed in the one true God worshiped by Abraham, new theological differences arose. Jesus spoke of the Godhead as having three aspects—Father, Son, and Holy Spirit—which we now call the Holy Trinity. His earliest disciples were also implementing new rituals called sacraments, intended to allow mortals to commune with God. This new spiritual path became known as "The Way."

Over time, several Christian beliefs proved incompatible with Roman life. The Romans had completely intertwined religion and politics, and everyone was expected to worship various gods and make sacrifices in the name of the deities to keep their favor. Everyone was also expected to worship the Roman Emperor as a god.

Christians did not object to praying *for* the emperor, but they would not pray *to* him or worship him, nor would they make sacrifices to the Roman gods or participate in pagan rituals in any way. Many early Christians incurred the wrath of local merchants, who relied on the product sales for these rituals; these merchants were among the first to report Christians to Roman officials.[19]

By the end of his rule in the early second century, Emperor Trajan had issued imperial guidance: Roman officials were ordered not to seek out Christians; however, if someone was accused of, and admitted to, being a Christian, a Roman official would demand both sacrifices and prayers to a Roman god. If the Christian still refused—which Roman officials saw as stubbornness—they were convicted by their own admission and executed for blasphemy.[20]

Despite sporadic persecutions, Christians continued to worship and recruit new followers. By around 170 AD, there were some one hundred thousand Christians within an empire of about sixty million.

While pagans were accustomed to living for the fruits of this life, early Christians were living for glory in the next. Each Sunday, Christians gave offerings voluntarily, not mandatorily—out of generosity, not obligation.[21] The alms collected were used to support the poor, widows, orphans, or any other in need.[22]

Christian worship was open to all, including women and children, free men and slaves. Societal status held no bearing. All were welcome, yet inclusion wasn't automatic. Aspiring Christians had to first learn about the faith, often being assigned a mentor to guide them. After a long training period, those who were deemed sincere would receive baptism.[23]

Persecutions were sporadic but they didn't simply disappear. Christians were blamed for the Roman Empire's many misfortunes.[24] By the mid-third century, imperial persecution had ramped up and Roman forces seized Christians' properties, destroyed their homes, and burned their texts. Faced with heavy persecutions, Christians moved their services to catacombs—underground passages which led to burial chambers for the dead.

When Sainte Foy was born near the end of the
third century, anti-Christian sentiment became
inflamed once again. Emperor Diocletian's sooth-
sayers could no longer read their omens,[25] and
Galerius, commander of the army, convinced the
emperor that the gods were angry. He blamed the
Christians, who were five million in number by
300 AD—about one-tenth of the empire.[26]

Investigations ramped up, and persecutions
followed. Enforcement was more aggressive along
the eastern empire and in Northern Africa, but
Gaul was affected as well. The conflict inevitably reached Agen, where Foy's life was forever
altered.

Foy, whose name means Faith, was born into
a wealthy family. As a young girl, she was raised
by her nurse to be a Christian, but this was done
in secret, unbeknownst to her parents. She developed a reputation as a sweet, playful girl with
fair skin, rosy cheeks, a pretty face, and a kind
heart—one who helped care for the poor and
lepers of the city.

When she reached the age of twelve, Foy was denounced during an imperial investigation, and she had to face judgment in front of a Roman council. Her parents had already come to realize by then that she was a Christian, but at the onset of the trial, they expected she'd renounce her beliefs and receive only a slight reprimand.

Foy was brought to trial in the public square. The prefect called her to stand in front of the tribunal. When the prefect asked the girl to state her faith, Foy confessed she was a Christian and had been from her earliest youth.

The prefect urged young Foy to abandon such beliefs. He then asked her to make a simple offering by taking just a few grains of salt and incense and then drop them on the altar to honor one of the Roman deities—he recommended Diana, a goddess who looked favorably on women. Foy, though, did not budge.

He implored her to think of her parents and the grief they'd be spared. With this small offering, she could return to them and soon be ready to take a bridegroom, raise a family, and live a blessed life.

Foy replied, "I want to take pleasure in my Lord (Jesus Christ), it is with Him I want to laugh and be gay, it is Him I would take as bridegroom, whether it pleases you or not; for to me He is fair, to me He is altogether lovely. I will not lie: If I cannot have Him, there is nothing that will heal me."[27]

With her head high, Foy then spoke to the entire council and to the huge crowd in the square, saying, "Your gods and goddesses are but demons. They are evil spirits," and "There is but one God."[28]

Foy's words enraged the prefect, but he gave her one last chance—renounce her faith in Christ, or perish. Sensing what awaited, Foy accepted her fate to become a martyr, to receive the victory crown of eternal life. "No, I will not sacrifice to Diana, nor will I touch your incense."[29]

The prefect called for the guards to take her. Young Foy's clothes were ripped off, and her naked body was beaten mercilessly. Her arms and legs were shackled to the corners of a brass gridiron bed, which was then lowered over a brazier of flaming hot coals.

Once the flames began to burn her flesh, the fire inexplicably extinguished itself. The confused guards dragged Foy's still-conscious body off the grill, and one of them, with one swipe of his sword, chopped off her head.

Several other Christians went on to receive martyrdom that day, but Foy was the first. Afterward, the surviving Christians took the bodies of the dead and hid them outside the city.

Persecutions like this persisted throughout the empire, but the tactics did not produce the desired effect. Pagan hearts grew weary of such methods, and—unlike the early days of Christianity—the communities knew who these Christians were, and what deeds they stood for.

Diocletian stepped down due to illness, and soon after, Constantine, a Caesar favorable to the Christians, rose to power. After Constantine defeated Maxentius at the battle of Milvian Bridge, he became emperor of the western half of the empire.[30] In 313 AD, the Edict of Milan was passed, promising freedom of religion throughout the Roman Empire.[31] A decade later Constantine became ruler of the entire empire, a position he held until his death in 337 AD.

Back in Agen, local Christians were now free to worship as they pleased. They built a beautiful basilica dedicated to Sainte Foy, and her relics were recovered and moved into a marble mausoleum, where she was venerated.

While holy martyrs are said to receive the reward of divine inheritance of everlasting bliss within God's kingdom, they also become an instrument for miracles here on earth. In Sainte Foy, Agen had a Holy Virgin martyr. As the locals honored her, her basilica began to receive reports of healings and blessings. Hearing of them, people ventured to Agen from far and wide in hopes of being on the receiving end of one of the miracles that seemed to flow abundantly from her shrine. Such devotion to the holy martyrs became known as the Cult of Saints.

Christianity rapidly expanded through the empire. By 360 AD, thirty million people had accepted the tenets of Christianity.[32] Twenty years later, it became the official religion of the Roman Empire. Yet in the fifth century—Rome's twelfth in existence—the empire collapsed. The emperor's edicts went largely ignored by the political class, and then by anyone who could get away with it. Within the first decade of the fifth century, the Roman military could no longer uphold its borders, and Germanic tribes like the Visigoths and the Vandals pushed across the Rhine.

While barbarian pressure mounted, the structure of Roman society imploded. Military posts were abandoned, taxation and inflation spiked, and the middle class collapsed. Without the protective force of the military, law and order crumbled, pillaging surged, education ceased, and medical knowledge was lost. As Roman civilization fell apart, multitudes were forced into lifelong enslavement by Germanic tribesman and slave traders.[33]

The eastern half of the empire survived, becoming known as the Byzantine Empire; its capital was Constantinople (modern-day Istanbul). In the west, large Roman estate owners held onto what they could, but the Germanic tribes took possession of much of western Europe. Many groups developed their own protectorates, providing residents protection in exchange for labor and produce; these great estates grew into small kingdoms. Antiquity was ending. Christendom was on the horizon. The Middle Ages was set to begin.[34]

ILLUMINATION

Conques came into existence in the eighth century, when a hermit named Dadon ventured along the Dourdou River and discovered an undisturbed valley nestled within the rugged hills, finding it a peaceful place to meditate. Thinking the valley resembled a shell, he named it Conques, from the Latin root "concha."

By this time, the Visigoths had been forced out of Gaul. They were pushed down to Hispania (Spain and Portugal) by Clovis I and his Franks, who ruled Gaul as part of Francia for over two hundred years.

Christian asceticism grew over that time as well. Disillusioned with a worldly existence, some seekers left society and went to live in woods or caves. Some ascetics went out into the desert wilderness and lived in solitude in northern Africa, focusing their thoughts on God to overcome the temptations of the flesh. They became known as the Desert Fathers and Mothers, and their example led to a monastic movement in Francia as well as on the Italian peninsula, where Saint Benedict founded the first Benedictine monasteries.

As Conques attracted more seekers, a monastery was founded to follow the Rule of Saint Benedict. It was an autonomous community, living under the authority of a single abbot chosen by its members, with a philosophy focusing on prayer, work, and study.

Benedictine monasteries were always centers
for learning. They dedicated as much time to
reading as they did to work, and up in Conques,
there was no shortage of the latter. An easy life
didn't exist in these hills, but, believing that their
work developed humility, over many years the
monks built this place up stone by stone to create
a celestial village.

While the monastery was still young, the
monks desired to increase the abbey's status.
They decided the best way to do so was to find a
saint, and it was Sainte Foy and her miracles that
inevitably caught their attention.

They devised a plan to send one of their own
to Agen to become a part of its holy community, which cared for the tombs of several saints.
When the time was right, the monk would steal
her relics and bring her back to Conques. Their
logic was that if the Sainte Foy didn't want to
come, then she wouldn't allow their plan to work.

The chosen monk left Conques for Agen, and
slowly won over the trust of the holy order there,
becoming a guardian of Sainte Foy's shrine. After

a decade of service, one night this monk placed her bones into a bag, snuck out of Agen, and successfully carried her relics all the way to Conques. Sainte Foy must not have minded; she was said to have healed a blind man along their journey.

Once they arrived in Conques, her remains were laid to rest in a reliquary. The monks and villagers became devoted to her, and she to them. Foy became their patron saint—and in such a rough age, they needed one.

Not long after, a man named Guibert came to live in a nearby village. He worked for a relative named Gerald, a priest and also his godfather; Guibert served him by managing his business dealings. On the eve of Sainte Foy's vigil, Guibert visited Conques, and after partaking in her feast the following day, began his journey home.

While in the wilderness, Guibert encountered his godfather Gerald with a small entourage. Gerald secretly harbored jealousy against Guibert, so after the men exchanged pleasantries and Guibert went on his way, Gerald had his men seize his godson. Gerald accused Guibert of wickedness, supposedly over suspicion of debauchery with a woman—likely Gerald's wife or mistress, as priests at that time could still marry.

Guibert claimed that there was some misunderstanding and pleaded for mercy, but Gerald savagely ripped his godson's eyes out and threw them on the ground. Suddenly, a snow-white dove (or possibly a magpie) swooped down, picked up Guibert's eyeballs, and flew off in the direction of Conques. Seeing this, Gerald immediately repented and began to weep, but the damage was done.

Gerald's own mother helped nurse Guibert back to health as best she could. The blind Guibert became a jongleur, and tried to adapt to a life without sight. Then on the eve of Sainte Foy's vigil the following year, Guibert fell into a deep sleep. He said he was visited in a dream by Sainte Foy, who told him that she pleaded to God and swayed Him to mercy. She told him to go to Conques for her vigil the next day and place one candle in front of the altar of the Holy Savior, and another one in front of hers. She said, "Do this, and your eyes will be wholly restored." Guibert thanked her profusely, and then she vanished.

The following morning Guibert went to Conques. With help from some monastic officials he was able to buy two candles and place them in front of both altars. At the vigil, he prayed ceaselessly by Sainte Foy's image, and at about midnight, he saw two globes—full of light, and about the size of berries—float across the room and travel deep into his eye sockets. The physical impact stunned him dizzy, and he passed out.

In the morning, he awoke in the church to the sound of the choir, which was already assembled and singing. Guibert stood up, but he could see only shadows. He was in great pain, and in a state of deep confusion. Finally, as the pain subsided, his vision returned. His eyes had been fully restored, and he and all who knew him rejoiced.

People had heard of the restoration of sight, but the re-creation of eyeballs after they'd been ripped from their sockets—*that* was new! Word of this incredible miracle traveled far, and Sainte Foy became even more beloved and celebrated.

Hearing of such otherworldly miracles, a cleric named Bernard got permission to investigate. He was a proud Christian, but he was very skeptical of the stories he heard coming from Conques. Bernard left his religious studies in Chartres, near Paris, and traveled south to this small village.

When he completed his long journey and arrived at the church, it was so packed he could hardly enter or kneel for prayer. Just as the monks had anticipated, people were coming from all over to see Sainte Foy. As he finally approached her shrine, he was shocked. In front of him stood a three-dimensional, three-foot-high golden statue. He could not believe it. "An idol!" he lamented.

Sitting on a throne was a human figure wearing an imperial crown and a gilded robe studded with brilliant gems, elegant pearls, and ancient cameos. Its golden face, though, appeared nothing like the pretty girl Sainte Foy had been described as. The head of the statue appeared to be that of a man—perhaps originally from another statue of some unknown ruler. The rest had been made specifically for Sainte Foy, and her skull had been placed within a wooden box inside the heartspace.

Such reliquary-statues were an ancient custom indigenous to this region, predating even Roman times; even today, many who have gazed into the hypnotic eyes of the figure have felt themselves staring into eternity. Bernard, however, was taken aback by such a representation. He feared that people were praying to the statue itself, which the locals called the Majesty of Sainte Foy. He later regretted such a sentiment, conceding that the reliquary-statue was not treated as Sainte Foy herself, but as a vehicle to her.

His skepticism toward her miracles soon changed as well. Bernard got to meet Guibert and interviewed many witnesses to the miracle of his eyes being restored. As Bernard heard of other reported miracles, he investigated them as well. He wrote down all he learned—and became a true believer in the process.

His writings left us with a view into the medieval world and Christendom's interwoven church and state. There was a rough nobility, who had their own vassals. They lived in castles, which had their own prisons.[35] This world knew all kinds of conflict, and the use of force was rampant. Attacks, feuds, ransoms, and church lootings were all common.

On the side of righteousness stood Sainte Foy, who played a large role in and around Conques. Along with bestowing healings and blessings, Sainte Foy settled land disputes and righted wrongs—and sometimes, she punished malfeasance. Local villagers loved her. The monks even took up arms against assailants to defend the monastery and protect her reliquary. Sometimes they were able to hide her statue from thieves or pillagers. Other times, they gave up their lives defending it.

Sainte Foy's influence extended well beyond Conques. Bernard observed countless chains hanging within the church. Upon inquiry, he learned that the chains were from prisoners who had prayed to Sainte Foy, asking her to free them and guide them to safety. When she responded, those she freed would walk to Conques just to lay their chains by her altar in gratitude. At one point, so many chains had been brought to Conques that the monks had to melt them down; the metal was then molded into doors to secure various entrances around the church.

Chains weren't the only things arriving here. Sainte Foy appeared to a French countess who desired a male heir; she requested the woman make an offering of her most cherished bracelets. After obliging Sainte Foy's request, the countess went on to bear not one healthy son, but *two*.

Sainte Foy often requested her devotees' most valued jewelry, testing their attachments to material things. Her devotees were careful not to go back on their word, though. If a piece of jewelry was promised to her and not delivered, Sainte Foy might simply take it herself—rings have been said to fly off people's fingers here.

In hopes of appealing to her penchant for pretty things, pilgrims continually offered Sainte Foy their finest gems and jewelry while praying humbly for her intercession. She captured the hearts and minds of so many that, at one point, over a thousand chapels were dedicated to her across Europe. A pilgrim haven in its own right, Conques also became an important stop on the way to Santiago de Compostela.

Through the rough Middle Ages, Sainte Foy never lost her playful side. Toward her devotees, she remained especially mischievous. One prisoner was promised his freedom, but during his first two escapes, he twice found a critical door locked, forcing him to scurry back into his cell so he wouldn't get caught. Finally, on his third attempt, Sainte Foy opened all essential doors, and at last he reached his freedom. These tricks of hers came to be called *jocas*.

Another story involves a warrior—a horse soldier—who developed an inguinal hernia, where part of his intestines dropped into his scrotum. Due to the pain of his condition, he could no longer perform his cavalry duties and was demoted.

Distraught, the soldier prayed to Sainte Foy, and she visited him with some peculiar instructions. Sainte Foy told him she'd help, but the soldier would have to visit a blacksmith, place his ailing sac over an anvil, and have the blacksmith hit the soldier's intestinal protrusion with his hammer.

The desperate man went to visit a blacksmith and managed to explain the request. But as the hammer came down to strike him between his buddies, the soldier fell back in fear. When he hit the ground, his intestines shot back into their proper position. The soldier claimed to suffer no more intestinal issues afterward.[36]

Through all the turmoil France was to face in future centuries, Bernard's book of Sainte Foy's miracles somehow survived, as did many religious gold-works of the age, including Saint Foy's Majesty statue. The entire area has remained connected to this Virgin Martyr. Church officials in the tenth century attempted to move her reliquary-statue to a more accessible church in Clermont-Ferrand, but try as they might, Sainte Foy's statue would not budge.[37] It's still at Conques, where she remains the patron for her people.

Tribulations

After a restful, hijinks-free stay within the abbey's old monastery, I follow the markers out of the village, leaving Conques as the rising sun bakes clear the morning mist. A cobbled path guides me along the edge of the steep wooded gorge and then descends sharply until reaching the River Dourdou, where a stone footbridge ushers me across the river before the painted markers guide me back into these rugged hills.

In a few days' time, we leave the hills of the Aveyron and begin traveling across the Lot Valley. This is a much flatter section of the Via Podiensis, a welcome relief at this stage of the

journey. Arriving at each place by foot, we continually meet new pilgrims. We find joy in the
simple things, like strolling old streets and
squares of Figeac, or savoring specialty pastries
and croissants in Cajarc.

To get a sense of what's to come, pilgrims
can refer to a Camino guidebook, which allows
us to plan each day's *étape*.[38] Reading about a
place is one thing, but seeing it for yourself is
quite another. Guidebooks simply provide some
context for what to anticipate; typically they list
the distances from town to town, as well as the
places where you can find accommodations and
basics, like food and water.

Guidebooks also inform us of alternate
routes to take. Some of these, such as the one
to Rocamadour, take days to complete. Other
detours only last a few kilometers, adding a more
challenging walk but offering better views than
the flatter, more direct route.

With no return ticket purchased yet for the
States, I have plenty of time to embrace this experience without feeling rushed. All that's important is right in front of me, and there remains

much to see. Along with a great number of French cottages, there are plenty of old chapels here, many of which are dedicated to Saint Roch, a French saint who's said to have cured medieval pilgrims of the plague by making the sign of the cross over their wounds.

It's easy to get distracted during these long walks. Deep in conversation with other pilgrims—talking about anything: family, hopes, dreams, spirituality, our lives—occasionally we'll lose track of the red and white markers. Without having any immediate clues telling us that we missed a turn, we just keep walking and walking, further and further along the wrong path. After some undetermined amount of time, one of us finally realizes, *Hey, there haven't been any markers lately. Hmm...* Now we have a choice to make: Continue onward hoping it's just paranoia, or backtrack until finding that last marker? Eventually we'll relent, realizing it's time for the latter.

As we draw nearer to Cahors, we travel along a stone-walled path going through thick forests. These waist-high walls accompany us through the woods for days on end. How strange it seems

to have any walls lining a path through a forest!
Time has worn these ancient barriers down; now
they appear mostly as long piles of white rocks
covered with thick clumps of green moss. Their
heights have become uneven because many of
the rocks from the top of the wall have long since
tumbled off and now lay along the trail.

This portion of the Camino is an ancient
Roman road. What was once a Roman supply
road has been repurposed and is used today only
by avid hikers or fellow pilgrims. This route was
supposedly even more isolated centuries ago,
attracting bandits; it was so dangerous that medieval pilgrims were told not to come through here,
forcing them to find other ways forward.

Everywhere a medieval pilgrim looked, they
would have faced another obstacle. The earliest
of them needed to forge their own paths. With
no painted markers or detailed maps, they nav-
igated using the sun and the stars. Some believe
we're following in the footsteps of a much older
pilgrimage, one that predates Christianity or
even the Roman conquest. It's known as the Via

Lactea, an ancient Celtic tradition of heading west, following the stars of the Milky Way, until reaching the waters at the end of the world.

The presence of ancient symbols and sacred dolmens along this journey only fuels such discussion. But while the two pilgrimages may overlap, there's no taking away from the works that Christians have left behind. They've displayed their own esoteric wisdom by embedding sacred geometry into the many churches and cathedrals along our way, and all across Europe. The medieval world built a whole network of pilgrimage paths traveling to various sacred destinations around the continent. Many of these trails lie dormant today, yet some are starting to reawaken.[39]

Medieval pilgrims came to view a pilgrimage as a way of coming closer to God; the act itself was believed to absolve past sins, and the more hardship one endured, the greater the amount of sin forgiven. A pilgrim who journeyed to venerate a saint might hope to one day emulate that saint's deep faith or lofty deeds; or maybe they looked to earn themselves a holy advocate in heaven to speak on their behalf.

In the Middle Ages, pilgrims walked for many religious reasons: to offer gratitude, to show faith, to serve penance, to gain favor, to ask forgiveness, or to request a miracle. Of the many pilgrimages, three were seen to have preeminence: Jerusalem, Rome, and Santiago de Compostela, where Saint James's body is said to still remain.

James and his brother John were fishermen whom Jesus led to become apostles. For their eagerness to fight, Jesus jokingly called them the Sons of Thunder, yet it was James, John, and Peter who formed Jesus' innermost circle. As his closest disciples, these three were the only apostles present during the Transfiguration, when Jesus' body turned to pure light. After the Last Supper, they were the only three with Jesus in the garden of Gethsemane, where he was arrested the night before his crucifixion.

When the apostles went out from Jerusalem to preach across the known world, James is said to have traveled to the Spanish peninsula to spread the Gospel. About ten years after Jesus' crucifixion, James returned to Jerusalem, and he was arrested by King Herod Agrippa and put to death by sword.[40]

After his martyrdom, legend has it that James' disciples took his body, brought it to the sea, and transported his remains via rudderless boat to the outermost region of the Spanish peninsula, to a place known as Galicia, where James had supposedly preached.

It was there that his body was laid to rest, yet his whereabouts were then lost until the early ninth century, when a hermit—living out west in the Kingdom of Asturias—saw a guiding star that led him to an ancient mausoleum containing several tombs. One was identified as Saint James, or Santiago as he came to be called by locals who began devoutly venerating the site.

Word of this discovery spread, and by the end of the following century pilgrims were venturing from all over Europe to visit his shrine. Each pilgrim's journey began at their own doorstep. Then they'd walk or ride horses through untamed lands for as many days or months as necessary until they reached the holy city.

Many early pilgrims never actually made it to Santiago; they died before they could complete their journey. The Church urged pilgrims to clear their debts and update their wills before even attempting the Camino, in preparation for the dangers ahead. After they began, some would succumb to sickness, falling to diseases such as the plague. Others might be defeated by nature, drowning while attempting to cross a rapid river. Some were bested by beast, stalked and killed by savage wolves. Others were ambushed by outlaws, robbed and murdered by vicious thieves for their precious coins.

The Church advised medieval pilgrims to not even carry money, suggesting instead that they rely on the charity of others on their journey. They were also advised to stay in churches, monasteries, and hospices to avoid sleeping unprotected out in the wild.

For the fortunate ones who did make it to Santiago, their journey was only half over. Once they arrived, they then had to prepare themselves—in

a world without planes, trains, or automobiles—
to walk or ride back home.

But through it all—in the face of uncertain
odds and an unknown future, in a time when
tragedy struck swiftly, violently, and frequently—
these ancient pilgrims found the courage to walk.
To advance, to go forward while death lurks, is
as noble a thing as I know, for a life where fate
goes untested is a life squandered.

During my journey, I've encountered no bandits,
staved off no wolves, caught not even the common cold, nor swam across a single river. I have,
however, crossed over many a built bridge, and
for these I am thankful.

I arrive at one such bridge during my early-
morning exit from Cahors. I make my way
through heavy fog to the western edge of the city.
Appearing through the mist is Pont Valentré, an
arched stone footbridge stretching a hundred and
fifty meters across the River Lot.

Three fifty-foot-tall towers fortify both ends of the bridge and its center. The bridge remains a throughway for pilgrims, but the towers used to serve as a defensive measure for the city. Although the bridge was never attacked, it didn't remain without story.

Major challenges to the bridge's construction popped up again and again, and—at some point during the seven decades it took to build—its foreman supposedly offered his soul to the devil in return for assistance in completing the perilous project.

The devil obliged and helped with the remaining construction. At last, with only a final stone needing to be set in the central tower, the foreman—fully realizing now what was awaiting him—gave the devil his final order. For the last batch of mortar to be mixed, the devil would have to carry the water up the central tower using... a sieve. The devil was unable to complete his task, so the bridge remained a single stone away from being finished, and the devil never got his due. Now, all these centuries later, the bridge is recognized a symbol of the city, and it's rumored that the devil can still be seen scaling its walls.

Centuries ago, a town's defenses were critical to its survival. Founders used nature whenever possible to protect their inhabitants. Sometimes that meant building alongside a major river, like in Cahors. Other times it meant building on top of a large hill, as in the case of Lauzerte, which I reached a few days later in my journey; yet others meant using water and elevation to protect themselves, as in Auvillar a day after that.

In the Middle Ages, attacks could come from anywhere. If the threat wasn't from a direct neighbor, then it could always come from the Vikings up north. And further south, in the eighth century, a new movement began spreading west from Arabia, across northern Africa. It eventually came up through Spain after several North African tribes defeated the Christian Visigoths, bringing with them a new Abrahamic religion called Islam.

While the appearance of these small towns has remained the same for centuries, times are always changing, and they've certainly done so along the Camino as well. Practically no one walks their return trip home anymore. Most pilgrims start not from their homes, but along one of the main pilgrimage routes like the Via Podiensis. While I've met a few pilgrims attempting to walk the entire way to Santiago—I even met a select number who had begun from as far back as Germany, Switzerland, and Austria—most European pilgrims today choose to walk their pilgrimages in increments. After walking for a week or two, they'll halt and return home to resume their normal lives. They'll then plan to come back the following year, pick up where they left off, and walk another section of their Camino. They'll repeat this cycle again and again until they are finally standing within Saint James' Cathedral, even if it does take them four, six, or sometimes ten years to do so.

Some folks today are less interested in walking an ancient pilgrimage and more interested in hiking a long-distance walking trail. They see their time here as a break from everyday life, a chance to walk quietly along the countryside while taking in fresh air and reconnecting with nature. And why not? Here they get to be their own boss, make their own schedule, walk any alternate routes they wish. Each person's journey becomes all their own, and how one chooses to walk it comes down to their time and resources.

For pilgrims in need of help today, assistance can be found in places called *donativos*. These establishments—usually run by eccentric gîte owners or devout religious orders who open their doors to all pilgrims—provide pilgrims accommodations without asking for a minimum donation. True donativos simply say 'Give what you can.' Then it's up to each pilgrim to follow their own conscience, because this system only works when those who have resources provide some for others with limited means. I've seen plenty already who dared to make the journey to Santiago without being able to afford the price of a contemporary gîte. Donativo sightings have been rare in France, though, appearing only every hundred kilometers or so. Pilgrims needing to further manage costs do so by cooking their own meals and sleeping in campsites whenever possible.

By week three, I've entered the Gers (formerly Gascony). Here we pass by a blend of sunflower, corn, and wheat fields sown over a region rich with rolling hills. In addition to the old chateaus adorning the landscapes, there are plenty of interesting sites like La Romieu, where you can learn about the local legend of Angeline and her cats.[41] A few days later, the Camino goes through Larressingle, the smallest fortified village in all of France; which has a three-hundred-meter ring perimeter, is protected by defensive walls, overseen by archer towers, and surrounded by moat.

Many of the towns in this region are built along a grid, with straight roads that intersect perpendicularly. At their founding, the locals cultivated the land outside these towns, and lived within their confines for safety. They're known as bastide towns, and on these cool October days, their vibrant streets are full of commerce. Their

center squares draw the most attention. Packed
with outdoor markets, these squares draw all
the townspeople, who can be found buying their
local produce, sifting through racks of clothing,
and perusing accessory items like caps and hand-
bags.

Off in the distance, I can finally see the majestic Pyrenees. The budding peaks span the horizon
now and are growing a little taller by the day.
Their presence becomes a daily reminder of just
how far I've come. Still, I must stay disciplined,
listen to my body, and walk my own pace, not
someone else's.

Not wanting to turn this into a race, which a
younger me would have surely done, I resist the
urge to rush to the finish. The Camino is a challenge, but it's not a competition. And no matter
how grand the accomplishment, the euphoria
always wears off. We'll always find another goal
to pursue later. It's better to focus on the here and
now, because our time out here is only as mean-
ingful as we make it.

I can imagine no better way of discovering a country than by exploring its countryside by foot. My French gradually improves. My pains occasionally subside. Walking up to a town is much more memorable than driving into one. Each day we get to see new places, drink delicious wines, and taste exquisite cheeses, which the French claim to have more varieties of than a calendar has days.

What I've appreciated most so far have been the subtle differences—the little things that to me are, well, foreign:

The French pronounce wifi as 'weefee,' an expression sounding better-suited for the name of a little old lady's lap dog.

During a toast, when your glass touches another person's, you always make eye contact with that person. *Always*. If not, tradition says you'll be cursed to seven years of bad sex. *Chin-Chin!*

At breakfast, places along the French country-side serve coffee not in mugs, but in cereal bowls. Anarchy, I say! Well, that *was* my sentiment, until the first cold morning dawned and I wrapped my hands around that smooth ceramic bowl with steam rising up. It warmed me as would a fire, and at that moment I got to know a little piece of heaven—and now on any future cold mornings, a mug simply won't suffice.

Coming to the Pyrénées-Atlantiques, the final region of France, the Camino cuts through a slew of farms with sweeping fields covered with green grass, perfect for the herds of cows and sheep spending their days grazing. Moving by rustic farmhouses, rocky trails guide us through thick forests, while small wooden bridges carry us over rivers, allowing us to go forward.

The further through France I walk, the fewer pilgrims I see. Several pilgrims have had to stop due to unfortunate injury, but most have simply returned home after walking a particular section. This late in the year, there are hardly any new faces popping up along my route. The number of pilgrims I see each day has dwindled significantly; I now cross paths with one, maybe two pilgrims per day.

France's walking season is closing out. Gîte owners are shutting their doors for the off-season, and they won't be reopening them until the coming spring. A few times I find myself being the gîte's final visitor of the year and feeling like I'm the last pilgrim walking. But I don't mind the solitude. In today's busy world, I find solitude can be a gift—a gift not enjoyed often enough; a gift, so I'm told, that will no longer be present once I've reached the more bustling Spanish portion of the Camino.

With the mountain chain just up ahead, we spend our final days in France moving over low-lying foothills and stopping by hilltop villages. On our last days in France, the rolling countryside brings us to the Basque village of Ostabat. Here the Via Podiensis merges with the Camino routes traveling from the shrines of both Sainte Mary Magdalene in Vézelay and Saint Martin of Tours. This joins three of France's four sacred routes heading to Santiago. The fourth one—coming from Arles, ushering in pilgrims from southern Europe along the French Riviera—won't meet up with us until a few days into Spain.

The Threshold

After a little over a month, and with just over five hundred miles to go, I finally reach the edge of the Pyrenees, coming to Saint-Jean-Pied-de-Port, a quaint fortified town nestled along the bottom of a large hill at the base of the mountains.

This eight-hundred-year-old town is less than a day's walk over the Pyrenees to the invisible Spanish border. Known once as a frontier fortress, Saint-Jean is still equipped with arrow-slitted stone ramparts that wrap around the northwestern portion of the hillside facing Spain, creating a crescent-moon-shaped perimeter along the base of the hill. It envelopes the original part of town to the hillside, fortifying its exterior, and protecting the houses and shops within, including the large, long-retired Citadelle sitting atop the hill some two hundred thirty feet above the town.

Like all pilgrims coming from France, I approach Saint-Jean from the east and arrive at a twenty-foot-high stone wall joined to the large hill rising up to my left. Cut into the center of the wall is a small arched passageway. The entrance is known as La Porte Saint Jacques (*the Gate of Saint James*), a special milestone for pilgrims. It marks the beginning of our follow-on route going across Spain. It was appropriately coined the 'French Way,' though it's best known by pilgrims as the 'Camino Francés.'

Stepping through La Porte Saint Jacques' open set of wooden doors, the arched gateway ends and a narrow cobblestone street begins. This quiet street, La Rue de la Citadelle, is lined on both sides with flat-fronted, three-story houses. Their exterior walls are all stuccoed white but have exposed blocks of the underlying blush-pink sandstone showing along their outer trim.

The cobbled street begins to bend, casually curving left to hug itself around the large hill. The street starts to descend to compensate for a downward slope. This forces the height of each successive building to drop a few feet lower than the one previous, creating a cascading effect for the ginger-red, mission-style roofs pieced into endless rows of barrel-shaped clay tiles lying just beneath the skyline.

Each building here shares a wall with the next, making this a seamless corridor, through which I can see a portion of the Pyrenees underneath the cloudy, mid-evening sky. Their green peaks are right in front of me now, just a few kilometers away. They continue to wait for me patiently, just as they've done since I first saw them a little over a week ago. But that's a journey for another day. For now, my attention comes back to this corridor to admire the simple yet charming façades along the street. Each one is equipped with a single entranceway secured by an old wooden door, and each level has a pair of windows complete with crimson-red shutters.

Engraved above some doorways are centuries-old inscriptions. Written in this area's native Basque language, I'm told they acknowledge the year in which a structure was built along with either the family name or, if it had been a business, the type of trade one could have expected to find within.

Continuing down the street, potted plants hang over many a windowsill and grace the thin walkways along both sides of the street. These walkways are very narrow, only a couple of feet wide, and are made of silver stone like the street. Every so often there's a step, built in to keep pace with the street's descent. There's no need to use them, though; there are no cars to contend with here. I simply walk in the middle of the street, moving around the occasional townsperson as I pass by little restaurants and local shops while searching for my gîte.

Humbled by the long journey, I arrive with a grizzled beard, sun-blistered ears, and a veteran's resolve. I've finally reached my halfway point. Of my journey's thirty-three days, I've walked thirty-two, but after having trekked 75 km over the past two days, any energy I once held in reserve is now drained—along with any chance I'll be walking 28 km up and over those mountains tomorrow, supposedly the most challenging day of the Camino.

Stopping here for my second rest day feels like as good a place as any. I'd stay longer if I could. This place exudes a certain *je ne sais quoi* that makes it a place one could live out an eternity or two.

A quarter-mile after entering Saint-Jean, the street begins to flatten out and I reach the bottom of the hill. About a hundred meters ahead, the corridor ends upon coming to a five-story tower stretched across the street. This tower, like the rest of the town, is built from local sandstone, though it remains un-stuccoed, showing its beautiful blush-colored blocks from top to bottom. The former—high above me—is accentuated by a large white twelve-hour clock face, while the latter—at street level—features another gate, which cuts through the tower. This western gate has provided passageway for centuries of travelers to and from Spain.

The tower is a couple of stories taller than both the face of the church connected to its left and the row of stores on the right, which form a small outdoor marketplace. The tower is probably the tallest built structure within the town, though it may not seem so since it's at the bottom of the hill.

Moving through the wide gate, I immediately come to the base of a forty-foot arched stone bridge extending across a gentle river running through the village.

Flowing north alongside the mountains and through Saint-Jean, the River Nive brings the town fresh water from the green-peaked Pyrenees staggered in the background. The footbridge under which the river glides leads to a street across the river, which in turn leads up the closest mountain.

Below the bridge, the river pushes north away from the town, flowing through the expansive valley covered with green patches of farmland

and pockets of white-washed buildings sprawled across the valley.

Walking over the bridge, I stop halfway and turn left for a chance to look over the river. The ground along the riverbank to my right lays flat, allowing several large homes to skirt the very edge of the river, their rear walls facing the water and extending down to the water's edge.

A dirt path runs along the left side of the riverbank. Just behind it, the hillside climbs straight up from the path to the hill's crest, where the retired Citadelle sleeps hidden behind a tall, green-leafed tree line.

I stare back out over the river and beyond the trees, taking in the view. The evening sky hangs lit up, blazed by the sunset into hues of pink and orange. The beauty of the sight is rivaled only by its meaning: that this moment is somehow meant for me, because some *thing*, for some reason, has led me to the Camino, which has led me to this town and now here, to this sunset— and although similar sunsets will follow, they'll never be exactly the same as this one. Since each is unique, in some small way, that makes this my sunset.

Truly though, by following life's signs, I'm assured of one thing: Of all the places in all the world, I'm right where I'm supposed to be. I need not fret about where I'm going, because I know I'm being guided, and I'll receive help as needed along the way. It's a notion that comforts eternally, like a mother's promise.

It's not enough to just believe in signs—you have to follow them. It's the only way to know you're on the right path. But once you do follow them, all life's moments become interesting and possibilities seem limitless.

I turn and continue to the far end of the bridge and onto the road that leads up the mountain. This road, La Rue D'Espagne, is lined with shops and houses similar to those on the other side of the river. It's almost a mirror image of the road I just came down, except that this road does not bend as it ascends; it travels in a straight line, and has no end in sight.

My work for the day is done. Not far from the bridge, I find my gîte. I check in, find a room and drop off my bag, and then take a shower. The rest of the evening is spent in relative leisure—I drink a beer, eat some dinner, and rest my feet, the pleasure of each activity amplified by every hour walked.

At night I lie down on my bunk, zip into my sleeping bag, and let the world fade away, sleeping soundly all through the night, hearing nothing at all—not the shuttering of any windows, not the squeaking of any doors, not even the snoring of any roommates. Absolutely Nothing. It's wonderful.

The next day I wake up smiling. My body couldn't be more delighted with my decision not to walk today—or perhaps this feeling is relief. Either way, the few pilgrims who stayed the night at the gîte have left shortly after breakfast. Usually, I'd be leaving along with them, but today I sit twiddling my thumbs, unsure of what to do.

I'm not one to lie around all day, so I decide to wander the streets of Saint-Jean. Stepping out of the gîte and back onto the cobbled rue, I find the town is already awake. In no particular hurry, locals stroll the streets and flow in and out of the local shops. Many of the men are in tweed jackets and sporting Basque berets, while the women are wearing long country dresses looking as if they're on their way to church. Quite fitting, actually—this is Sunday, after all.

As I move along, the scents from the food shops flood the streets as well as my senses. One by one they lure me in to taste their freshly-made croissants, crepes, and my newfound French favorite—mini cannelés, caramelized cakes with custard-filled centers. *Magnifique!*

I'm well aware that this is a lot of indulgence for a single morning, but one of the perks of walking so much is that these calories will not reach my waistline, an opportunity I find less and less with each passing year.

Afterward, I walk around doing touristy things: I visit a place called the Bishop's Prison, walk around the massive Citadelle, then take in the view of the mountains and the valley from high upon the town's looking point.

Ah, did I mention what it feels like to be walking without a pack on my shoulders all day?

It's glorious. It's as if gravity has somehow forgotten me, and I've become weightless.

Next I choose to walk the path along the river. Here I find time to reflect and refocus. Maybe I should feel a sense of accomplishment for reaching my halfway point, but I don't, not with such a long way still to go. Perhaps it's because I have a large mountain right in front of me. But after witnessing other pilgrims' Achilles tendons locking up and their knees giving out, I am no longer naïve as to the challenge still ahead. To date though, my pain has been just that—pain. And anyone who's ever accomplished anything can be no stranger to pain. So as concerns arise, I do my best to convert these sentiments into hopes, not fears. I hope my good fortune will continue; I hope my body can endure; and I hope I can persevere.

Perseverance: It's a trait the military forged into me, and is not to be confused with stubbornness, a trait I was born with. There can, however, be a fine line between the two, so I hope God grants me the wisdom to know the difference so I may reach Santiago in good health.

Enjoying a midday ice cream, I notice the next wave of pilgrims arriving. Some I've met previously and had passed while walking. Others, I can tell, are new pilgrims, arriving here most likely by train. All bright-eyed and bushy-tailed, they go around purchasing last minute items, mostly things they'll regret buying later for the added weight they bring. Tomorrow will be their first day—and for a few, if they haven't trained sufficiently, it will unexpectedly be their last.

THE
PYRENEES

Paradisio

[The Rise of Roland]

On the following morning, it's time to say goodbye to Saint-Jean-Pied-de-Port. I'm starting the Camino Francés by walking Route Napoléon, a path that leads up and over these mountains, delivering pilgrims to a retired monastery in Roncevaux, Spain.

Saint-Jean's cobbled rue ends, and a paved road begins leading me up the mountain. Both sides of the street have plenty of white-walled houses intermingled with thick patches of green forest on what becomes a steep country road with hardly a bend or a lull. It just keeps going and going, up and up.

I walk alone carrying my pack, a day's supply of water, and my lunch. As my muscles begin to burn, I keep my mind blank and my head down so as not to focus on the remaining distance ahead or on the clouds I intend to reach. Instead, I look toward the street a few feet in front of me and take one step, then another, and another. On and on this goes, and I develop a rhythm between my steps and breaths.

Gravity, the cruel witch, has returned with a vengeance. She clings to my back, making it clear she has no intention of leaving today. The higher I climb, the heavier she gets. With my quads feeling singed and my shoulders simmering, all I can do is dip my head down and keep pressing forward. To avoid blisters, I keep my feet relaxed, rolling each one heel to toe, heel to toe.

Hour after hour, the climb continues. By midday, the mountain bestows some mercy, and the slope softens. Up here, it's just grass-covered fields and a blacktop path slithering up the mountainside. There are no buildings up here, no trees. Aside from the occasional pilgrim walking, there are only flocks of grazing sheep and dozens upon dozens of auburn-bodied, blond-maned horses roaming freely.

Able to see far and wide now, I relax and peer over the neighboring mountains. Next I look back to France, taking in the expansive green valley below as well as the towns I so recently walked through to get here. Taking a moment, I bask in this world view—one usually reserved for birds. The challenge of getting here has made this all the more beautiful. So painfully beautiful.

Moving even higher, the climb becomes quite steep once again. The path veers off the paved road and continues along a dirt trail rising up through steep fields toward the mountain's crest.

Almost out of water but with several hours still to go, I come to some woods, where I'm fortunate to find a small, stone drinking fountain off to my left. *La Fontaine de Roland*, the final source of water in France, looks to be in the middle of nowhere, but it's actually the site of a great military battle. Way back in 778 AD, this is where Roland, a paladin of Charlemagne, fought and died within these woods at the Battle of Roncevaux Pass.

Historically speaking, very little has ever been found about Roland. Only one historical attestation actually proves he even existed: Charlemagne's biographer briefly mentioned the battle, stating that when the Carolingian rearguard made their way through this pass, they were ambushed. While protecting their king, the entire rearguard was slaughtered, down to the last man. Of the thousands killed, only three names were mentioned, and Roland's was one of them. He's noted as having been "Lord of the Breton March." And that's it.[42]

No other official document has ever been found to mention Roland, just that one reference in Charlemagne's biography. Yet in death, Roland was about to find new life. Tales of his extraordinary heroism became so well-known that Roland would one day be named the national hero of France.

I refill my water and continue into the rustic forest. The path now skirts a sloped mountainside that steadily rises up on the left side and drops far below me to the right. The forest is full of bizarrely shaped trees—some twisted, others curved—shooting high out of the sloped ground.

Close to the crest of this mountain, the elevation has fast-forwarded autumn. All the leaves have turned yellow or brown and have already fallen to blanket the ground, leaving the ash-colored trees and their high limbs bare with bark.

A light mist looms. I've been warned about the weather up here and how it can turn on you in a second, but for now visibility remains fine. At the time of Roland's death, this eerie wilderness marked the boundary between the Christian- and Muslim-ruled worlds. During the decades leading up to Roland's demise, major battles were being fought on the French side of the Pyrenees, with their outcomes likely deciding the religious fate of Europe.

After the invading North African tribes defeated King Rodrigo and his Visigoths in

711 AD, the Umayyad Dynasty seized control of nearly all of Spain. Once Spain was conquered, Muslim forces began invading Francia. The Frankish Dynasty had been in decline, but Charles the Hammer of Austrasia and his son, Pépin the Short, established the Carolingian lineage in its place.

After hard-fought Christian victories in Toulouse (721), Tours (732), and then Narbonne (759), the Carolingians successfully pushed the Umayyad expansion back to the far side of these mountains, allowing Pépin's son Charlemagne and the Carolingian Empire to rule the main body of Europe north of the Pyrenees, while Abd ar-Rahman I and the Emirate of Córdoba reigned over the entire Spanish peninsula to the south,[43] all except for the small Christian kingdom of Asturias, which controlled the uppermost northern strip of Spain.

During this decades-long conflict, pro-Abbasid Muslim leaders positioned closest to the Pyrenees were fighting with the Umayyad powerbase in Córdoba, and they looked to the Carolingian king for assistance.[44]

In a deal gone bad—where Charlemagne was promised the submission of the Spanish cities Barcelona, Huesca, and Zaragoza by the pro-Abbasid Muslims in exchange for military aid— Charlemagne and his forces were denied entrance into Zaragoza in 778 AD. The Muslim governor reneged on his promise with the Carolingians right outside his walls.[45]

In retaliation, the Carolingians immediately began a siege of Zaragoza to take it by force. One month into that offensive, however, they got word of a Saxon revolt in the northern part of their kingdom. Charlemagne gave the order to abandon the siege to go quell the Saxon uprising, and he also received a large tribute of gold from the Zaragoza's governor for lifting the siege.[46]

Charlemagne and his troops left Zaragoza and headed north toward Roncevaux. First they visited Pamplona, where they learned that the local Basque inhabitants had formed an enclave with the Muslims, who were also referred to as Saracens. Charlemagne ordered Pamplona's defensive walls torn down.

Traveling back to Francia, Charlemagne and the main body of his army successfully traveled through the high pass near Roncevaux, but as the rearguard followed, they were ambushed by a contingent of Saracens attempting to free one of their own military leaders,[47] along with the Basques, who were retaliating against Charlemagne for Pamplona's walls being destroyed.[48]

Likely surviving as a local story at first, tales about this battle were passed along by oral tradition for centuries, and eventually became immortalized as legend. An eleventh-century manuscript shows just how the story took shape in the nearly three hundred years since Charlemagne's biographer had briefly mentioned the battle.

This ancient text called *La Chanson de Roland* (*The Song of Roland*) describes the Battle of Roncevaux Pass in a four-thousand-line epic poem. Written in Old French, it is the oldest surviving major work of French literature.

The Roland emerging from this text has been given a full backstory: He now has an unbreakable sword called Durendal, a peerless horse named Veillantif, and a knightly companion in Oliver. He's made out to be both bold and brash, but in addition to being one of the Carolingians' top military leaders, Roland has now been elevated to be Charlemagne's nephew, with many creative edits still to come.

This poem opens by saying that, instead of having spent only a single season in Spain, Charlemagne and his troops have been fighting a full seven years there. They have successfully liberated all Spanish Christians from Muslim rule, except for those in Zaragoza, which is portrayed as the Saracen's last stand. (In reality, Zaragoza had been as far as Charlemagne's forces ever actually advanced.)

The poem never mentions the Basques. Instead, the impending attack on the rearguard is set in motion by a betrayal from within Charlemagne's own court. (The traitor's name is Ganelon—and he was Roland's own stepfather.)

With the Carolingians camped just outside the city, King Marsile, the ruler of Zaragoza in the poem, realizes his forces are doomed, so he and his council devise a plan and offer a truce. King Marsile will provide Charlemagne's forces with a large tribute of gold, and the Carolingians will depart for their capital of Aix-la-Chapelle. King Marsile further pledges to follow shortly behind them, traveling to Aix to renounce his faith, receive baptism, and become a Christian. (He has, of course, no intention of actually keeping his word.)

Charlemagne considers the offer with his own council, and they contemplate whether or not King Marsile can be trusted. Roland speaks out against the proposal, preferring to take the city by force. However, the remaining eleven council members, including Roland's stepfather, Ganelon, are all in favor of accepting the truce; everyone is ready to return home after fighting for seven years.

Charlemagne decides to accept King Marsile's offer, and wonders whom he should send to finalize terms. Roland is one of the first to volunteer, but he is deemed too brash for such a sensitive mission. Roland suggests that his stepfather would be a fine choice, but Ganelon is enraged at having been volunteered for what he considers a dangerous duty.

Charlemagne, though, agrees with Roland and chooses Ganelon to deliver final terms to King Marsile. Ganelon immediately curses Roland and vows vengeance against him, though the council dismisses his outburst without any thought of him actually being a traitor.

When Ganelon arrives—alone—to the negotiations, he spreads fear among the Saracens, convincing them that they'll never truly be rid of Charlemagne as long as Roland, the king's favorite knight and nephew, is by his side. Believing this, the Saracens agree to conspire with Ganelon to ambush the rearguard and destroy Roland.

With the tribute of gold and riches secured, the Carolingians begin their journey back to Francia. Instead of stopping in Pamplona, the poem has Charlemagne's forces leaving Zaragoza and heading directly toward Roncevaux. While Ganelon rides alongside Charlemagne in the formation's main body, Roland and Oliver take charge of the rearguard, leading twenty thousand French knights.

The army's vanguard and main body successfully navigate through Roncevaux Pass, and descend into Francia. As the rearguard moves along the same route, Oliver spots a horde of Saracens—a hundred thousand fighters—heading toward them. He implores Roland to sound his oliphant horn to notify Charlemagne so he'll know to send them reinforcements.

Fearing neither death nor great odds, Roland refuses—he even welcomes battle in hopes of showing God how prepared they are to suffer great hardship for their liege lord and king. He also believes their own might will be enough to propel them to victory.

Convinced that the rearguard will be overwhelmed by the sheer numbers of Saracens, a more prudent Oliver pleads with Roland again to sound his oliphant. But nothing Oliver can say will change the mind of the more prideful Roland, who believes that sounding his oliphant now will put the king's life in undue jeopardy, and could only be seen as an act of cowardice.

Thinking him arrogant, an angered Oliver scolds Roland, but to no avail. An archbishop named Turpin rides up alongside them and intervenes, saying the moment for arguing has passed; the fight is now inevitable. The knights all dismount and take a knee. The archbishop says a prayer to absolve them of their sins, then tells them their penance will be to strike hard against the approaching enemy. The knights all leap back on their horses and begin shouting King Charles' battle cry—*Montjoie! Montjoie!*—until the sound reverberates throughout the pass.

The mêlée begins with Roland riding out on Veillantif, his swift courser. He charges toward the oncoming Saracens and lifts his lance to strike the first blow. The strike is a powerful one: Roland not only pierces his opponent's shield and armor, making a hole in the man's body, but the impact flings the Saracen a full lance length off his horse.

Riding "like a baron" alongside him is Oliver, who strikes the next blow by stabbing a Saracen through the breast. Oliver's lance and pennant are thrust through the soldier's body before the man is thrown lifeless to the ground.

It turns out Archbishop Turpin is a warrior-priest, and the next strike is his. He rides into the fray and his lance point splits Saracen steel. He then shakes his opponent off his spear, dropping him dead to the dirt.

The battle continues, with the French knights inflicting more casualties against the larger Saracen force. The poem's descriptions of the battle allow time for the knights to engage in spirited discussion in the midst of battle. The two sides spend most of their time hurling insults at one another and shouting slurs—heathen, infidel, villain, felon.

A few Saracen fighters are depicted as being noble and courageous, but most are portrayed as nasty and traitorous men. Throughout the poem, Christians and Muslims show a mutual hate and distrust toward each other—which was indeed how these two groups felt toward one another when the poem was penned. Around the end of the eleventh century, Christians and Muslims were about to battle for control of Jerusalem. It was a conflict framed as a Holy War, pitting Cross against Crescent, Christian against Muslim, in what became the First Crusade.

Both sides believed their faith to be the True Way to salvation; both thought themselves to be fighting in the service of God; and both were willing to prove it on the battlefield, where God's will could best be shown—because both agreed it's God who grants the victory.

God is said to favor those who conduct themselves with honor and dignity, and on the field of battle, a person shows themselves to be valorous by bravely facing death. In the poem, the Christians and the Muslims are said to be fighting well in a battle described as both "marvelous and grievous," with both sides striking terrific blows.

After many strikes with his lance, Roland finally draws Durendal, his mighty sword, which contains relics of the great saints. On Veillantif, Roland charges at the closest Saracen and slices him through from scalp to horse, and both go tumbling dead.

Roland, Oliver, and the other knights continue carving and stabbing their way through this crowded battlefield, which is covered with the bodies of the dead and dying. The knights thoroughly trounce the hundred thousand Saracens—to the point that only two remain.

But just as the French knights begin to grieve their fallen, King Marsile appears with three hundred thousand more soldiers. Roland urges his men to be strong and asks them to stay and fight, for just beyond these hordes will be Paradise.

The new battle rages with the Christian knights standing firm, but now it's the Saracens beginning to inflict most of the carnage. The knights, though fighting valiantly, lose their lives one after the other, after the other.

When only sixty knights remain, Roland now feels compelled to blow his oliphant to, at last, notify Charlemagne. However, his friend Oliver rebukes him again, saying it would be a shameful act at this point, as it would serve only to save themselves. He then begins pressing blame on Roland and chiding him for his reckless nature and lack of prudence.

Archbishop Turpin stops Oliver once again, this time telling Roland that he *should* blow the horn—not in hopes of saving themselves, but so Charlemagne can avenge their deaths and retrieve their bodies for a proper burial.

Roland agrees with the archbishop, and begins blowing his oliphant with all his might. The horn sends an incredible burst of sound through the ether, one that can be heard some thirty leagues away. But Roland exerts such force in sounding the alarm that the veins along his temples burst, leaving him mortally wounded, blood running out of his mouth.

Outside Roncevaux Pass, Charlemagne and his troops do hear Roland, but Ganelon tells them to dismiss the distress signal, assuring the king that his favorite nephew is likely just out

hunting. Ganelon's insistence raises Charlemagne's suspicions, however, and when a soldier
rides up and confirms that Roland is in trouble,
King Charles orders Ganelon put in chains to
be dealt with later. The king and his soldiers go
racing back to the pass to aid Roland and his
knights.

In the pass, a barely-conscious Roland looks
over the fallen and prays for God to welcome all
his brave knights into Paradise. Then, while he
has any life left in him, he resumes fighting. Soon
after, he cuts off the sword hand of King Marsile,
who then flees the battlefield.

Oliver is soon stricken from behind through
his armor. His deep wounds cause him to lose
his vision, and amid the battlefield confusion he
comes close to stabbing Roland. But Oliver collapses, and the two amend their lifelong friend-
ship as Oliver takes his last breath.

As the last two Christian knights left standing, Roland and Archbishop Turpin continue
trading blows with the Saracens until—at last—
the distant trumpets of Charlemagne's forces are

heard echoing through Roncevaux Pass. This frightens the remaining Saracens into fleeing, leaving Roland and Archbishop Turpin on the verge of death.

Both are bloodied and beaten, but Roland and the archbishop find the strength to start gathering the bodies of some of their fallen comrades. Roland faints from exhaustion, and the archbishop goes to bring him water. Before he can accomplish this, however, Turpin drops dead. Roland awakens and sees the archbishop lying lifeless. He then carries Durendal and his oliphant up to an open field and comes to a tall tree. He collapses next to it.

Fearing Durendal may fall into the wrong hands, Roland stands and, with all the lifeforce left in his body, raises his sword and begins hacking at a marble stone beside him. But try as he may, Roland fails to make a chip or even a nick in the unbreakable sword.

Unable to destroy it, Roland lies back down and tucks the sword underneath him. He begins dreaming of fair France, knowing he will never again see it in the flesh. Once more he prays for God's mercy and asks for his sins to be forgiven. For his final act of fealty, he holds his right glove up to the heavens. As Roland's life expires, his hand falls upon his chest, and three archangels descend upon him to carry his soul off to Paradise.

Charlemagne and his forces obtain vengeance by chasing down the hordes of fleeing Saracens and killing them. The poem then depicts one last battle, where the Christians are victorious and fully liberate Spain. Once Charlemagne and his men are back at their capital of Aix, Ganelon is put on trial and convicted of treason. The council sentences him to one of the most gruesome known forms of medieval execution. Ganelon is quartered—each of his limbs is bound with rope, and his body is ripped apart by four horses.

The events of this poem came to define Roland's legacy. Stories of Roland and the rearguard would be told and retold, and his song would spread throughout the continent. Manuscripts of the Song of Roland have been discovered all across Europe, with at least eight of them surviving today. All vary to different degrees, yet all revolve around what transpired within Roncevaux Pass.

The character attributes portrayed by Roland made him the quintessential knight of the Middle Ages. The poem presented Roland and his knights as heroes, while promoting the values of service and sacrifice as well as faith and loyalty.

His legacy resonated throughout the Middle Ages. Just as King Arthur and Lancelot were central to the literary cycle of the 'Matter of Britain,' Charlemagne and Roland were the main figures of the 'Matter of France.'

These French poems were tales of historic figures wrapped in Christian folklore. Passed along by their ancestors, they were called *chansons de geste*—songs of heroic deeds. They shared the sacrifices of their forefathers, giving them examples to emulate. They also warned aspiring knights of the type of tragedy that might befall them, and taught the knightly code of conduct called chivalry.

In search of a good death, they instructed, a person should start by living for others. This was an ideal embodied in chivalry, which—at its origins—meant to act nobly, to give generously, and to protect resolutely those unable to protect themselves, such as orphans, widows, and the elderly.[49]

These were just some of the ideals passed along, but poets can only plant the seed. For virtues to blossom, they must be nurtured. This responsibility falls mostly on family. There to deal with the day-to-day upbringing of their children, parental figures have the challenging role of raising fine sons and daughters, establishing in them a sense of right action, and teaching them to carry themselves with dignity and to hold themselves accountable for their own deeds. Nonetheless, even the wisest mentor can only show a pupil the path; it's up to the individual to walk it. While we are all fallible, and the most talented tend to be the most troubled, we can still strive to be the best version of ourselves.

For centuries, Roland's name appeared in literature. Five hundred years after Roland's death,

Dante—who himself had walked the Camino—
wrote *The Divine Comedy*. In the fifth sphere of
heaven, sure enough, there was Roland, along
with Charlemagne, in the sacred space reserved
for holy warriors.[50]

In the eyes of the medieval world, Roland's
actions preserved the life of his liege lord and
king. While Charlemagne did not actually free
Spain from Muslim rule, his forces did return
a few years later and seized control of the lands
all along the Spanish side of the Pyrenees, which
became known as the Spanish March. The gar-
risons installed there strengthened the Carolingian Empire against the Umayyad Caliphate, and
thwarted potential threats from their Islamic
capital of Córdoba.

By continuing the work of his father and
grandfather, Charlemagne's military campaigns
reunified most of Europe three centuries after
the Roman Empire dissolved, preserving Christianity and its teachings as the prevailing religion
across Europe. For his success, in the year 800
AD, Charlemagne became the first Holy Roman

Emperor, and was later considered the Father of Europe.

The Carolingians brought Pamplona into their empire as well, even though its Basque inhabitants had partaken in the actual Battle of Roncevaux Pass. The Carolingians' relationship with the Basques remained fraught, but after Charlemagne absorbed the lands around Pamplona into his Christian sovereignty, his empire shared a border with the Christian Kingdom of Asturias. Asturias stretched all the way across northern Spain to Galicia, where Saint James' tomb was discovered just two years prior to Charlemagne's death in 814 AD.

Having created a seamless passage through Christian lands, this shared border made possible this very pilgrimage. It allowed the Christian faithful to make their way to the apostle's newly discovered tomb. Later legends would even go as far as to say that Charlemagne had actually liberated Saint James' tomb, subsequently founding this pilgrimage.

Grand tales about Charlemagne and Roland still thrive deep in the heart of Europe, shared and amplified over the centuries by the many pilgrims making their way through Roncevaux Pass on their way to Santiago. Since the Camino's founding, the lore around it has always remained tied to the campaigns of Charlemagne and Roland. Their lives were lifted up to the mythological realms, forever intertwined in legend. But every legend has its beginnings, and Roland's was right here in these woods.

After making my way through the pass, I finally come to the crest of the mountain and let out a sigh. With all the climbing behind me, the hard work should be done. I can just coast in from here, right?

Wrong. This turns out to be one of those times when going *down* a hill actually feels worse than going *up* it. Here, the western slope drops off like a dive bomber; the weight of my pack is not only pushing me downward, but now forward as well.

I struggle to keep myself and my pack from tumbling down the mountainside; the added, unwelcome pressure on my knees makes them feel like they're about to burst. Most pilgrims these days use walking poles to help keep the pressure off their knees during the journey. For whatever reason, I've never really wanted them, but now for the first time I actually regret not having them. Unfortunately, I see no helpful sticks lying around the forest to go pick up.

In order to compensate, I modify my path down the mountain by veering from one side of the path to the other, making an S-shaped swerve pattern like a skier going down a ski slope. This slows my descent a bit until the terrain begins to level out, at last. At this point, the leaves are all green and back on the trees again, unlike the bare-limbed branches up in the pass.

The forested path ends, and I come to an empty paved lot. On the far side stands a hundred-meter-long stone wall, five meters high, with gothic buildings connected to both ends.

There's a tourist information sign posted next to the wall, and I approach it to see where I am.

The sign has a layout map depicting the small cluster of medieval buildings that make up the village on the other side of the wall. For the first time, all the writing is in Spanish—a good sign. Really though, I'm concerned about one thing: What's the name of this town? Looking… looking… Ahh, 'Roncesvalles.' Oh, thank God— that's Roncevaux in Spanish. Bruised but not broken, I have arrived, completing what's considered the most challenging day of the Camino.

With the day in the books, it's time to rest and relax now. Tomorrow, we have another long walk ahead.

SPAIN

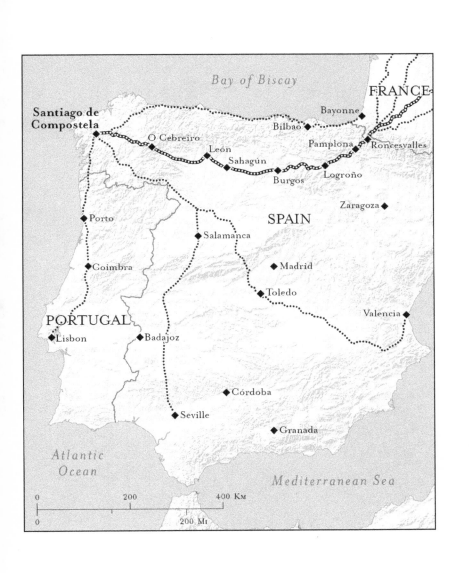

Bay of Biscay

FRANCE

Santiago de
Compostela

Bayonne

Bilbao

O Cebreiro

Pamplona
Roncesvalles

León

Sahagún

Logroño

Burgos

Zaragoza

SPAIN

Porto

Salamanca

Coimbra

Madrid

Toledo

Valencia

PORTUGAL

Lisbon

Badajoz

Córdoba

Atlantic
Ocean

Seville

Granada

Mediterranean Sea

0   200   400 Km

0   200 Mi

Conflict

Continuing the journey into Spain, I descend out of the mountains and into the Navarra region. The landscape here becomes very different from what I saw in France. The green rolling hills have been replaced by smoother prairies. The countryside is covered by a sea of pale-gold grass and there are far fewer trees, meaning far less shade. Thankfully for me and my Irish skin, this is less a factor now, in late October, than it would have been in, say, July.

Just as I had been forewarned, many new pilgrims have emerged along the Camino Francés; it's now normal to see pilgrims walking throughout most of the day. Eager to walk, these new pilgrims have brought the Camino a new energy— and found themselves new foot problems. Unlike back in Le Puy at the start of my Camino, most everyone here is planning to walk the entire way to Santiago, which can be completed in about a month's time.

If I had wanted more solitude, I suppose I could have chosen a different route. Perhaps I could have walked the Camino Norte running west along Spain's northern coast. If I had traveled north from Saint-Jean-Pied-de-Port, rather than west, I could have joined the Camino Norte in four days' time. At this point in the year, I could have practically walked it alone—just me and nature—seeing only a few pilgrims each week.

While busier and more commercialized, the Camino Francés has a more historic appeal. Sharing the road with more pilgrims shouldn't be too grand a challenge; besides, there's only so much to be gained from isolation. People enrich our experiences too.

In France, pilgrims were *pèlerins*. In Spain, we are *peregrinos*. As the landscape changes, our daily routines have changed in Spain as well. We now follow little yellow arrows pointing the way to Santiago, instead of the red and white dashes found on the Via Podiensis. The towns in this section of Spain are closer together than I saw in France, so it's now normal to pass through five or six per day. These small pueblos are typically simple farming towns. If we stop at all, it's to fill up on water, or maybe enjoy a cafe con lèche while resting our shoulders a bit.

Instead of gîtes, we now stay in *albergues*—a similar concept, though accommodations are even more basic. Depending upon the day, we arrive at the albergue either in the afternoon or evening. Once checked in, the top priorities are always a shower—which is sometimes cold—and washing clothes, often by hand.

After wringing our clothes out and hanging them to dry, the remaining time is ours. With only a half-day or an evening to explore, all you hope for is to make a memory—some moment to hold on to. For me, moments like this come as I wander under the balconies along the streets of Pamplona, share in midday drinks at an unexpected festival in Viana, or received a blessing from a bishop at a special mass in Logroño.

The next few days are spent walking through La Rioja. Autumn has painted this region's famous vineyards in shades of butterscotch, burgundy, and bronze, making it some of the most scenic walking yet. Spanish villas overlook the path from the region's sun-drenched hills; there's such a vast number of vines planted all around that you'll start to believe the locals' claim that they mix their concrete with wine and not water.

Moving along, we visit old churches and listen to more long-toothed legends. Just below this stretch of the pilgrimage is the site of the legendary Battle of Clavijo, said to have taken place in 844 AD. While the main body of Europe found religious stability by the ninth century, the conflict in Spain was far from over.

The Clavijo legend says that King Ramiro I of Asturias was angry about a certain tribute he was expected to honor: a hundred maidens each year, sent to the emir in Córdoba. These maidens were then taken as wives or sold as slaves, which was an agreement made a century prior, meant to prevent the more powerful Muslim realms from raiding the smaller Christian ones along the northern peninsula.[51]

Muslims had little economic interest throughout the Christian north; however, La Rioja was a wealthy region which held important trade routes. King Ramiro is said to have called upon all his Christian knights, and they marched against Muslim forces here in La Rioja. However, they found themselves faced with an innumerable army led by Emir Abd ar-Rahman II himself.

King Ramiro's Christian army was thoroughly routed. Afterward, he and his troops found shelter in Clavijo Castile near Mount Laturce. That evening a vision of Saint James appeared to him, telling the king to fear not. The apostle told Ramiro that he would be with them on the battlefield tomorrow—riding a white charger and holding a white banner—and would provide divine protection for Ramiro's troops.

The following day, King Ramiro once again led his Asturian army into the battle. In the midst of the fight, a great white knight appeared, seated on a white horse and carrying a white banner. He struck the field like a ray of light to sway victory toward the Asturians.

This legend—like Charlemagne founding the Camino—can be traced back to three centuries after the supposed events. There is no historical evidence of any large battles in Clavijo at that time, but the story does resemble the accounts of battles from the *following* decade—conflicts between King Ordoño I, Ramiro's son, and Musa II, a powerful ruler from a Hispano-Gothic family who had converted to Islam.

As in the legend, the first battle was won by the Muslims, but it took place in the year 852 AD. Excavations have found evidence of much of this fighting—however, it took place not in Clavijo, but in Albelda, its next-door neighbor. The second battle took place in 859 AD, and was won by the Christians by Mount Laturce, the very site of the Clavijo legend.

Though the legend condenses a seven-year conflict into twenty-four hours—with the decisive victory going to Ordoño rather than his father, Ramiro—the result remains the same. Christians from the north took possession of the region and kept hold of it thereafter, which is why the Camino has traveled through La Rioja ever since.

Since those early centuries, Spanish Christians have prayed to Saint James for protection. He was eventually declared the patron saint of Spain, and became a symbol of Spanish resistance to Moorish occupation. This earned him the new nickname Santiago Matamoros, or Saint James the Moorslayer.[52]

Each morning, the lights of the albergue go on at seven a.m. It's time to wake up, collect our gear,

and prepare for the day. Spain, like its neighbors, has its own inspired culinary culture. For
breakfast, we enjoy tortilla de patatas (hot, crus-
tless egg & potato pie), or tostadas con tomate
(toasted baguettes with blended tomato, a pinch
of salt and drizzle of olive oil). Add the morning
café, and we're ready to go.

Once full, we lift our packs over our shoulders and venture out into the cool morning air.
We walk west as the sun comes up, warming us
from behind as it ascends into the mid-morning
sky. Small pueblos appear along the horizon. The
yellow arrows lead us through fields up to these
little villages, whose tallest point is always the
church steeple. Once inside, we tour the pueblo's promenade, viewing its old-world treasures—
statues, monuments, coats of arms—still on
display. Eventually, we'll follow the yellow arrows
again, leading us to the next village.

I knew little about the Camino or Spain's
history when I began, but I'm learning as I go.
Each day is a moving history lesson, and each
place gets to tell its own story. Some of these sites

would never have existed if not for the Camino. When you stop in Santo Domingo de la Calzada, you see a place that was an untamed wilderness, until one man dedicated his life to building a bridge, hospital, and causeway to aid pilgrims along their journey. Eventually other buildings went up, businesses moved in, and a town was born. Named for the man so instrumental in building it, the town still lives on for us to walk through today.

Communicating has been much easier for me in Spain—my Spanish, while not good, is *mucho mejor* than my French. Interactions with locals remain limited; they either love pilgrims or seem indifferent to us. Beyond a little small talk, you can usually get a good restaurant recommendation out of them.

For lunch, we usually order bocadillo sandwiches, or perhaps some pinxos or tapas in the late afternoon. With plenty of cured meats and fresh cheeses to choose from, it's not hard to keep the palate happy. Lunch remains one of the most fulfilling events of the day, a good time to refuel and take a temporary respite to rest our aching bones and bodies.

We do a lot more walking along streets on the Camino Francés than we did on the Via Podiensis—and they're not always of the picturesque variety, either. Entering the region of Castile, someone thought it would be a good idea to have the pilgrim path run alongside a major highway for several days. A constant drizzle forces us to trudge along in our rain gear; the passing trucks make a resounding shriek as they roar by on the adjacent, water-soaked roadways.

Near Villafranca, we've reached what seems like the first set of woods since having left the Pyrenees a week ago. While walking through Montes de Oca, a gravel path takes us up and over rolling hills full of pine and oak forests, bedded with heather and fern. It's nearing November now, and most of the foliage has turned brown and begun to wither away. Reaching a clearing, we pass by cow pasture fields, followed by some rugged terrain where rocks seem to bubble up out of the ground.

Our daily walks continue to finish before sunset. As each of us arrives at our nightly destination, we're all eager to throw off our packs. After washing up, there's usually one thing on everyone's mind.

For dinner, local restaurants offer a special pilgrim menu, or the managers of the albergue offer a meal. Castile is known for its sopa de ajo (garlic soup), yet you can't go wrong with ordering fabada (bean stew) or lentejas (lentils), with or without the chorizo. Due to an influx of pilgrims here in Spain, we have many more communal dinners. Five or ten of us will typically work together to prepare our own feast. We'll all go to a local *tienda* and pick up a variety of foods—usually some assortment of breads, cheeses, pastas, salads, desserts—and yes, of course, the wine. There's always lots and lots of wine… just be ready to walk the following morning.

I've mostly met international pilgrims walking along the Camino Francés. We quickly learn to let the French or Italian pilgrims do most of the cooking. With both cultures having such deep cooking roots, the food they whip up tastes as good as you'll find anywhere.

These meals bring us all together, as only food can do. We sit together and enjoy meals like a family, passing dishes around the table, filling each other's cups with wine, and engaging in friendly conversation. We may have begun the day as strangers, but we don't have to end it that way.

After such long days, it's nice to sit and share stories as we let our bodies heal. While most of us speak English, it's common to hear three or four different languages spoken around the table at any given time.

The pilgrims here haven't just been from nearby countries like France, Italy, and Germany. Some are Eastern European, from countries like Poland, Czech Republic, and Ukraine. A few have even ventured here from further east to walk the Francés—from the likes of Russia, South Korea, even Australia. Some have even come from the far west Americas, from places like Argentina,

Brazil, Canada, and a few of us from the U.S. of A.

It doesn't really matter where anyone is from. While we share the common goal of reaching Santiago, we continue to form a special camaraderie. This is aided in part by the Camino having removed us from our normal existence. Whoever we thought we were off the Camino means very little now. Here, we are all pilgrims—no more, no less. This is never more evident than at bedtime, when we all walk into our shared, barrack-style room to lie down and sleep on bunk beds spaced about a foot apart. In normal life, people build barriers between one another, but the Camino breaks them down, leaving us with just the essentials—each other.

Then, as each morning comes and the sun rises, it's time for us to go—on to the next town. Onward to Santiago.

The Revenant

[The Return of Rodrigo]

Entering the city of Burgos, half the day is spent walking through a busy industrial zone. So long, trees. So long, fields. Hello, factories. Hello, office buildings. Along a four-lane highway, gridlocked cars roll by as we walk mile after mile along concrete sidewalks. Having been removed from city life for so long, every sensation feels amplified: the sound of honking cars; the smell of gaseous fumes; the heat reflecting off the pavement. All are reminders of a life I knew well, but right now it feels like I'm walking through some foreign land.

Once we reach Burgos' historic district, a much more inspiring scene appears. Here the streets bristle with medieval architecture. The old plazas and ancient alleys now bustle with bars and bistros. The main square hosts a magnificent cathedral capped with hollow spires which tower over the city. This surreal structure, both from the inside and outside, looks as if it's on loan from heaven, and we have somehow been granted a special viewing.

Burgos is about a third of the way across northern Spain. A city known for gastronomy today, it was once the historic capital of Castile. Burgos— and to a larger extent, the Kingdom of Castile— came into prominence around the middle of the eleventh century, at the height of the Christian-Islamic epoch, and the history of the two remains forever linked.

It was a world of kingdoms and conquests, where power and influence were wielded by nobles and faith leaders, when wars and feuds were settled with swords and on horseback. The eleventh century was also a time of religious and political turmoil in Spain; a great upheaval was about to take place, and a heroic warrior was about to emerge.

The end of the tenth century—nearly three hundred years since the North African Muslims had invaded and subdued the once-Christian peninsula—was one of the more peaceful periods. The era, reigned over by Abd al-Rahman III, has been described as *La Convivencia*. General religious tolerance existed between Muslims, Christians, and Jews, resulting in advancements in art, science, and architecture. But below the surface, these three religious groups still harbored a lot of animosity toward one another.[53]

Islamic Spain—known as al-Andalus, or Andalusia—was united under the Caliphate of Córdoba. The Muslim regime was the dominant force over the region, controlling most of the peninsula. The Muslims had ruled for so long that more than seventy-five percent of the pen-

insula had become Muslim.[54] To keep the peace
with the Muslim-held south, Christian kings
to the north had to pay tribute to the stronger
southern regime. But when al-Mansur became
the caliphate's ruler, the peninsula's fragile peace
was soon lost.

Al-Mansur had risen to power by wiping out
all of his political adversaries within the caliphate. While maintaining absolute power in the
south, al-Mansur continually organized raids
into the Christian north. He brought in North
African Berbers and even enlisted Christian mer-
cenaries to help him wage war, offering them a
share of the spoils. The most valuable commod-
ity was, of course, the enslaved prisoners of war.[55]

Directing his attention northward, al-Mansur
ignored his philosophers and went on to deci-
mate every major Christian center. In addition
to laying waste to many churches and monasteries, he destroyed Barcelona, Pamplona, Burgos,
León, and Zamora, and even captured Coimbra
out west. In all, his exploits amounted to over
fifty military campaigns, all of them victorious.[56]

Then in the summer of 997 AD, al-Mansur marched his army to the upper northwest, to the city of Santiago de Compostela. There his forces raided the holy city and burned it to ashes, including Saint James's shrine. Al-Mansur left the remains of Saint James unharmed, but he removed the bells from the smoldering church and forced captured Christians to carry the bells on their backs some five hundred miles so they could be hung as oil lamps in the Great Mosque of Córdoba.

From Santiago de Compostela's ashes rose a national fervor more determined than ever to reclaim the entire peninsula from Muslim rule. As the various Christian kingdoms rebuilt their cities, they also strengthened their forces and became better organized.[57] The reclamation movement became known as the *Reconquista*.

Not long after these destructive raids by al-Mansur, a remarkable reversal of fortunes came to pass. After razing La Rioja in 1002 AD, the sixty-year-old al-Mansur died of an unspecified illness. Absent a strong successor, the caliphate fell into civil war; and in less than thirty years' time, it splintered into self-interested, individualistic taifa kingdoms. Conditions on the peninsula would change so much that these taifa kingdoms of Muslim Spain—with their centers known for the arts, sciences, and the general pleasures of their palaces—would begin sending tribute to more austere Christian kingdoms so as to keep them at bay and to ensure their protection against any neighboring aggressors, both Muslim and Christian alike.

By mid-eleventh century, the most powerful Christian leader was King Ferdinand, who controlled Castile, León, and Galicia (roughly the same lands that had previously made up the Kingdom of Asturias). King Ferdinand received tribute from many of the taifa kingdoms, and reclaimed lands previously lost to al-Mansur decades prior. A devout king, Ferdinand also invested in his kingdom by rebuilding castles, monasteries, and churches, including breaking ground on a new cathedral for Saint James in Santiago de Compostela in 1060 AD.

In Ferdinand's kingdom, a young Rodrigo Diaz began moving through the ranks as a Castilian knight. Rodrigo had been born in a little town called Vivar, just north of Burgos. His family was of modest nobility, and it was assumed that Rodrigo would become a knight, but amid Spain's great upheaval in the eleventh century, he was destined to play a central role.

BANISHMENT

Fated as a youth to be schooled under the banner of King Ferdinand's eldest son Sancho, Rodrigo excelled at arms. While Ferdinand had three sons and two daughters, Sancho and his siblings, most notably Alphonso, acted more like rivals than relatives. It was Rodrigo and Sancho who developed a close kinship.

Near the end of his reign, King Ferdinand announced his intention to split his kingdom between his three sons upon his death. Sancho would receive Castile; his brother Alphonso would get León; while Garcia, the youngest, would receive Galicia. Ferdinand's two daughters Urraca and Elvira would, if they refrained from marrying, retain control over the monasteries in all three realms. The king's decision to partition the kingdom did not sit well with his sons, as each preferred to be the sole ruler of all three realms.

When King Ferdinand died in 1065, it didn't take long for infighting to begin. Conflicts arose between the three brothers in the kingdoms of Castile, Leon, and Galicia, and there were other conflicts that included the Christian kingdoms of Navarra, Aragon, and the county of Barcelona. These six Christian realms fought between themselves for control of the frontier lands; for tribute payments from the taifa kingdoms; and over the lanes of reconquest of Muslim-held territory.

For such disputes against Castile, King Sancho had to his advantage a young Rodrigo Diaz, who had distinguished himself on the field of battle. Rodrigo first won several duels in single combat, which traditionally showed that justice was on the victor's side. These early triumphs brought Rodrigo great honors from the Spanish people, who gave him the name Campeador, or 'Champion.'

A dispute over an outstanding tributary payment arose between King Sancho and the long-held Muslim kingdom of Zaragoza. King Sancho ordered Rodrigo to besiege the kingdom, and Zaragoza was so helpless against Rodrigo's tactics that the tribute was promptly restored in 1067 AD, and a treaty signed to affirm Sancho's overlord status. Rodrigo so elevated his reputation during the siege that the Muslims of Zaragoza began referring to him as El Cid, derived from al-Sayyid, meaning 'the Master.'

When Rodrigo was in his mid-twenties, King Sancho made him Alférez—the royal standard-bearer, leader of the king's army. Soon after, Sancho and Alphonso teamed up and removed their younger brother Garcia from power in Galicia. Sancho and Alphonso briefly tried to co-rule Galicia, but it didn't take long before tensions flared between them, and the brothers chose to settle their disputes on the battle-field. Their forces met in 1068 on the Llantada plain, and then again near Golpejera in 1072. Both battles resulted in victory for Sancho and his young general, Rodrigo. During the second battle, Alphonso was captured and brought in chains to Burgos. Sancho moved his brother to a monastery in Sahagún, but at the urging of their sister Urraca, Alphonso was released and sent into exile, finding refuge at the famed Alcazar of Toledo, the large Muslim kingdom of central Spain.

Sancho's reign over his father's three realms lasted all of nine months. A revolt broke out in León in the city of Zamora, held at that time by Urraca. Attempting to quell the uprising, King Sancho and his forces besieged the city. During the siege, a Leonese knight snuck into the king's quarters, found a lance, and used it to pierce San-cho's chest, killing the king in his own camp.

At the age of thirty-four, Sancho was dead. With no heir of his own, his power transferred to his next of kin—his exiled brother Alphonso.

Just like that, Alphonso's fortunes had flipped. The Castilians suspected that Alphonso, his advisors, and Urraca had conspired in the murder of Sancho, but nothing could be proven, so Alphonso returned and took control over León, Castile, and Galicia.[58]

Considered a capable leader, Alphonso ruled his kingdom under the banner of law and order. Like his father, he invested in the churches and monasteries in his realms. He also removed costly tolls imposed on pilgrims and built up the pilgrimage road traveling to Galicia, and in 1075, King Alphonso began construction of a grand cathedral at Santiago de Compostela, which still stands today.

Rodrigo Diaz pledged his loyalty to Alphonso, who accepted him as his vassal. But Rodrigo was now in a precarious position. With each of his victories, Rodrigo's legacy had grown, but two of those wins had come at the expense of Alphonso and his loyalists, whom Sancho had forced into exile.

Rodrigo now found himself further down in the pecking order with King Alphonso than he had been under Sancho. While the king arranged a favorable marriage for Rodrigo with his own Leonese cousin—Jimena, daughter of the Count of Oviedo, Diego Fernández—Rodrigo was stripped of his military post as Alférez. Rodrigo mainly served Alphonso as an ambassador or judge dealing with legal and religious affairs. With his military career sidelined, Rodrigo supposedly served his king well, but he still had enemies in court who he'd beaten in battle or were jealous of his fame.

Then, in the summer of 1081, some bandits from Toledo's northern frontier attacked and looted Gormaz, an important castle along Castile's southern border. Rodrigo led a retaliatory raid into Toledo; upon returning with many captives and cattle, he was met by an infuriated King Alphonso.

Rodrigo's raid had been unsanctioned, and his actions came at a volatile time for Toledo. King Alphonso had just fought to reestablish Toledo's young king, who went by the name al-Kadir, meaning 'the all-powerful,' although he would prove to be anything but.

Those who were envious of Rodrigo spoke out against him, and Alphonso's mind was successfully poisoned against the Campeador—who had, after all, defeated Alphonso twice. While Rodrigo felt his actions were justified, Alphonso sided with the dissenters, and he banished Rodrigo from his kingdom. By the end of that year, Rodrigo departed Alphonso's dominions, leaving his wife, two young daughters, and son behind. Rodrigo and his retinue rode out into the unknown, unsure of what was to come.

After being refused by the royal family in Barcelona, Rodrigo and his knights found refuge in the Muslim held kingdom of Zaragoza. King al-Muqtadir remembered Rodrigo from his siege of Zaragoza years prior, and retaining a warrior of El Cid's caliber seemed like a good investment to him.

King al-Muqtadir died shortly after Rodrigo's arrival. The king chose to partition his kingdom, leaving Zaragoza to his eldest son, al-Mu'tamin, who also inherited Rodrigo's services. His other son, al-Hāyib, was given the smaller, neighboring kingdoms of Lerida, Tortosa, and Denia.

It wasn't long before a bitter falling-out took place between these two brothers, and Rodrigo was asked to defend Zaragoza. Rodrigo went on to successfully thwart a siege of Almenar by al-Hāyib and his Christian allies from Barcelona. Remaining undefeated in battle, Rodrigo showed he hadn't lost his talent for swaying the outcome of war.[59] From this point on, Rodrigo became a thorn in the side of al-Hāyib and Spain's eastern Christian nobility.

In addition to being a fierce warrior, Rodrigo made a habit of insulting powerful men. In 1084, al-Hāyib went to Sancho Ramirez, the Christian king of Aragon and Navarre, and complained that Rodrigo had been harrying the countryside of Tortosa, near Morella. Thinking Rodrigo a menace, King Sancho joined al-Hāyib, and they rode out to confront him.

Once they found his encampment, they sent an envoy to El Cid, demanding he leave his position and never return. Rodrigo tauntingly replied to the king of Aragon that if his majesty and his troops would like to cross through the territory peacefully, then he, Rodrigo, would allow it. To further provoke the king, Rodrigo even said he'd provide them a hundred knights as protection to ensure a safe journey.

An enraged King Sancho and al-Hāyib attacked Rodrigo the next morning, in what turned into a long and hard-fought battle. In the end, Rodrigo's much smaller force withstood the onslaught, while Sancho and al-Hāyib's forces fled, which allowed Rodrigo's men to sack their baggage train. To the victors went an enormous treasure. Of the two thousand troops who were taken captive, Rodrigo set them all free without ransom—except for the seventeen highest-ranking nobility, known as *grandees* for their grand stature.[60]

This success elevated Rodrigo above all others. His resounding victory won him great honors and riches, and he was exalted throughout the kingdom. But even with all his triumphs, after three years in exile Rodrigo seemed no closer to receiving a welcome home. King Alphonso was showing little desire to end Rodrigo's banishment, for he was in the midst of forging his own legacy.

King Alphonso capitalized on more misfortune in Toledo, as its leader al-Kadir was struggling there once again due to constant uprisings.[61] Al-Kadir realized he had little chance of keeping his kingdom, so he reached out to King Alphonso. They came to a secret agreement whereby al-Kadir would turn over the throne of Toledo in exchange for Alphonso's assistance in reinstalling al-Kadir as ruler of Valencia, a small flourishing kingdom along Spain's eastern coastline, whose inhabitants had thrown off al-Kadir's lordship when he came into power in Toledo.

To starve any extremist factions of the city into submission—and to salvage the military honor of those about to lose a capital city renowned for its invincible natural defenses—Alphonso began to lay siege to the capital in 1084 AD. After a rough winter, the city officially surrendered to him on May 6, 1085 AD.

This marked the biggest moment of the Reconquista. Toledo was more than just the central kingdom of Spain. It had been the Visigothic crown jewel, the ancient capital of the Christian Visigoths ruling after the Romans, yet it had remained under Muslim rule for nearly four centuries.[62]

While Christians rejoiced over Toledo's reconquest, its fall sent shockwaves throughout all of al-Andalus. If Toledo and its impregnable defenses had fallen, surely it was only a matter of time before their own kingdoms suffered the same fate.

King Alphonso was proving unstoppable and had little need for the Campeador. There wasn't a single taifa ruler strong enough to oppose the king; Alphonso extracted large tributes from each of the taifa kingdoms and even installed lieutenants into nearly every one of their courts.

King Alphonso soon moved his permanent residence to Toledo. He next wanted to conquer Córdoba to the south. He claimed he could never rest until Santiago's church bells were rescued from Córdoba's mosque, where they had hung, being used as oil lamps, for nearly a century.[63]

Instead, King Alphonso and his forces headed east and began a siege of Zaragoza, attempting to conquer the Muslim kingdom. Rodrigo had no interest in fighting Alphonso. Even in exile, the Campeador still considered King Alphonso to be his sovereign, and his family still dwelt in Castile. During the siege, Rodrigo was said to have removed himself to a remote castle of the kingdom.

Several distraught Muslim kings crossed the Mediterranean to Africa, where they met with Yusuf ibn Tashfin, ruler of the Almoravids, who controlled the vast Muslim empire along northern Africa. They told Yusuf about Alphonso's harsh treatment and then asked Yusuf and his army to come and raise a Holy War in Spain, contingent upon him swearing an oath not to despoil them of their kingdoms. [64]

The taifa kings' request came with plenty of risk. The Almoravids had a reputation as great warriors; however, they were known to practice a very strict form of Islam, one which forbade many of the enjoyments found in al-Andalus.

Back in Spain, the siege of Zaragoza was taking its toll. Zaragoza's king offered to pay King Alphonso to leave, but Alphonso refused anything but a full surrender. Then on June 30, 1086, just as Zaragoza was on the verge of capitulation, the Almoravids arrived from Africa to take their first steps on Spanish soil. Though recent converts to Islam, these desert warriors—who wore lithams to cover their faces—were the most devout, most disciplined Muslims of the day.

Alphonso got word of the Almoravids' arrival, and he reached out to nearly all the Christian kingdoms in the regions of Spain, France, and Italy for assistance. Just about all of Christendom was called on—all except Rodrigo, who remained idle in Zaragoza.

Having no choice but to abandon his siege, Alphonso tried to accept the payment Zaragoza had previously offered. However, Zaragoza's king had already heard that the Almoravids had arrived, and he now gave Alphonso nothing.

A confident Alphonso marched the Christian troops west across Toledo and into Muslim-held territory. Leaders of the taifa states joined forces with the Almoravids at the capital of the Kingdom of Badajoz, and now King Alphonso and his forces marched to Sagrajas, just five miles from the Muslim capital.

On the day of battle, the Christian vanguard charged the Muslim front, which was made up of Spanish Moors. The Christians quickly overran them, and it seemed Alphonso's forces were winning the day. Yusuf and his army, however, were watching patiently off to the side. Despising the laxness of their religious practices, Yusuf regarded these Spanish Moors to be as much his enemies as the Christians, so he allowed them to kill each other for a while.

As the Christians began to tire, the Almoravids fell upon their rear camp. Alphonso attempted to turn his forces around to engage them, but the Christian forces were met with innovative assaults, in which the Almoravids synced their movements using flags and drums. During battle, the drum noise shook the ground and frightened the Christian soldiers' horses.

The two sides fought throughout the day. Finally, after great losses on both sides, the Almoravids routed the Christian forces and sacked their encampment.

In defeat, Alphonso and his remaining knights limped back home. As proof of their great victory, Yusuf ordered that the heads of all the slain Christians be lopped off and sent to the Muslim kingdoms all across al-Andalus. The Spanish Muslims were so impressed with his victory that they declared Yusuf 'Prince of the Faithful,' and then abandoned their tributary payments to Alphonso.

GLORY

After his victory, Yusuf went back to Africa to grieve the loss of his son who had just died of sickness in Cuenta. He left three thousand horse soldiers behind in al-Andalus to serve the taifa kings. As painful as Alphonso's defeat had been, he did not lose any territory—but his defeat did make him reevaluate his treatment of Rodrigo, whose banishment he finally lifted in 1087 AD.

Rodrigo assisted King Alphonso in reestablishing the king's supremacy along the eastern taifa provinces, but Yusuf returned to Spain in 1089, and he and the taifa kings began to besiege Aledo—an important southern outpost for Alphonso. The king and Rodrigo were supposed to link up along Alphonso's ingress to Aledo, but Alphonso took a different route, leaving Rodrigo and his troops waiting for Alphonso to pass them.

Due to endless quarrels and disunion between the taifa leaders, Yusuf decided to abandon the siege. Afterward, those still hostile to the Campeador convinced Alphonso that Rodrigo had purposefully held his troops back so Alphonso would be slain by the Almoravids. Believing this, an irate Alphonso imprisoned Rodrigo's family. Rodrigo was refused a hearing to defend himself, and although his family was soon set free, King Alphonso banished Rodrigo from his dominions once again.[65]

Rodrigo returned to eastern Spain. His previous experience in Zaragoza had taught him the interworkings of Hispano-Arabic politics and Islamic law, knowledge that would serve him well. Now as Rodrigo rebuilt his retinue, he negotiated with eastern taifa provinces to protect them under his own banner.

In Valencia, al-Kadir heard of El Cid's return to the region. He allied himself with Rodrigo, paying him tribute for protection against his many detractors. This included his neighbor al-Hāyib and his Christian allies, who all were working to destabilize al-Kadir's regime, but Rodrigo successfully stymied them, and established his own authority over the eastern provinces.

Yusuf and the Almoravids soon returned to Spain for the purpose of reclaiming Toledo. The Almoravids began besieging Alphonso's capital with the help of the Spanish Moors; however, after more bickering and dissention between the taifa kings, Yusuf abandoned the siege and did what he had sworn an oath not to do: He began despoiling the taifa kings of their kingdoms, getting Islamic clerics to issue fatwas to provide justification for his orders.[66]

Granada and Malaga fell to the Almoravids by late summer 1090; Seville and Córdoba by early summer 1091. Almeria, Murcia, and Denia fell by late 1092, as did Alphonso's most important southern outpost, Aledo. The taifa kings began to look to King Alphonso for help, but each of Alphonso's attempts to counter Yusuf's aggression was checked by the Almoravids, who continued consolidating power across southern Spain. Alphonso had no answers for the new tactics of these desert warriors, syncing their troop movements with flags and drums; meanwhile, his most capable general remained banished from his kingdom.

Toward the east, Rodrigo met with King Sancho of Aragon, and they settled their differences and became allies. Rodrigo then brokered peace terms between the kings of Aragon and Zaragoza, and all three entered into a pact against the Almoravids.

While Rodrigo was viewed favorably by the Muslims in his own retinue, as well as those in Zaragoza, other Muslims in al-Andalus despised him for harrying their countryside. They considered him a threat to both Islam and their way of life. Many wanted the Almoravids to rule, and actively sought to promote that outcome.

While in Zaragoza, Rodrigo got word of trouble in Valencia. Al-Kadir, as unpopular there as he had been in Toledo, had worn out his welcome. In late October 1092, the city's Qadi (chief magistrate), ibn Jahhāf, secretly led pro-Almoravid Valencians into revolt and took control of the city. Dressed as a woman, al-Kadir tried to escape, but he was caught and beheaded. When

Rodrigo arrived at the city gates, ibn Jahhāf refused Rodrigo entry, denying anything was even wrong. Rodrigo assured the Qadi that al-Kadir had been slain, and he would not rest until he brought the murders to justice.

Rodrigo began a blockade of Valencia in an attempt to starve the fortified city into submission. Enveloping it, he stopped all movement in and out of its walls. Valencia's food shortages began to mount through winter and spring. Yusuf sent a letter to Rodrigo telling him not to dare enter Valencia. The Campeador responded to Yusuf with a scathing letter of his own; then he wrote to all the leaders of Spain telling them that Yusuf—out of fear—would not come and fight him.

In August, Rodrigo freely offered the Valencians a one-month truce, lifting the siege after nine months. If Yusuf could defeat and expel Rodrigo by the end of August, then the Valencians could serve Yusuf. If not, Rodrigo asked the Valencians to serve him. The Valencians agreed, and they sent messengers to Yusuf and

to all the kingdoms of al-Andalus.[67] Yet when
Yusuf did not come, the Valencians went back on
their word and would not surrender, so Rodrigo
reestablished the siege.

A contingent of Almoravids finally did come
that November—without Yusuf—yet they left
without engaging in battle, crushing the Valencians' hopes. During the next winter, food shortages within Valencia's walls took such a toll that
people were dying of starvation. With no sign of
assistance from the Almoravids, the Valencians
finally relented and entered into final terms of
surrender to Rodrigo that spring. After a struggle of nearly twenty months, on June 15, 1094,
Rodrigo had conquered Valencia.

Rodrigo's family soon joined him in his newly
acquired kingdom. Under the terms negotiated
with the Valencians, Rodrigo restored land to its
owners and allowed them to continue their own
religion, laws, and customs. He chose adminis-
trators from all three Abrahamic religions, and
outlawed the keeping of slaves within city walls.[68]
He also taxed them according to what was pre-

scribed by their faith, an amount similar to a tithe, which was a great reduction from what their own Muslim leaders had been forcing upon them.[69]

The Almoravids conquered Badajoz out west that same year, completing their takeover of all the taifa states to the west and south. In just four years, they had conquered all of al-Andalus up to Valencia. They were proving invincible, and the only thing standing in the way of them taking the remaining eastern Muslim provinces was the Campeador, who was heard saying that while one Rodrigo (back in eighth century) had lost the Spanish peninsula, another Rodrigo would save it.

Determined to take Valencia for themselves, the ever-victorious Almoravids arrived to do battle with an immense army in the fall of 1094. Yusuf did not come, but his orders did: Capture Valencia, and bring back Rodrigo, alive and in chains. The Almoravids encamped along the plain of Cuarte, just four miles west of the city. Their soldiers swarmed the perimeter, banging their war-drums and shooting flaming arrows over the city walls while shrieking and yelling taunts to provoke a fight.

Rodrigo requested help from King Pedro of Aragon and King Alphonso, but neither could offer much in the way of support. Outnumbered, and with no help on the way, Rodrigo calmed his retinue and prayed to Christ for nine days. On the tenth day, he seemed to get his answer. In a bold move at dusk, his cavalry shot out the front gate while Rodrigo and another band of knights charged out a lesser gate. The opposing vanguards clashed as Rodrigo and his horsed knights stormed undetected around the Almoravid formation. In a flash, Rodrigo and his men's lances fell upon the Almoravid's rear camp. They fought until their lances broke, then laid into the Almoravids with the sword.

With the two vanguards locked in battle, Rodrigo's attack on the rear camp created such surprise, such havoc, that the far superior number of Almoravids could neither gather their wits nor rally. The battle turned into a rout and the Almoravids fled, abandoning their camp. Invincible no longer, the desert warriors had suffered their first loss on Spanish soil. To the victors went the spoils of unfathomable wealth, and the win erased the notion that the Almoravids were somehow unbeatable.

With the Almoravid aggression checked, Rodrigo returned to rule his kingdom. He demanded fealty from all those under his banner, and ordered that all ties to the Almoravids be cut.[70] After an investigation, ibn Jahhāf was arrested for orchestrating the coup that resulted in the death of al-Kadir. He was found guilty and sentenced to death. Rodrigo asked Valencian officials what their custom was for punishing murderers of kings. "Death by stoning," was the Valencian's response, but they emphasized that it was Rodrigo's choice, his decision. "For us," Rodrigo said, "it's burning."

Soon thereafter, ibn Jahhāf was buried up to his chest, a fire was built up around him, and he was burned alive.

King Alphonso continued to have little success against the Almoravids, suffering defeat after defeat against them in battle. Rodrigo, however, was victorious against them once again at the Battle of Bairén. The Almoravids briefly pinned down Rodrigo and his knights, but Rodrigo foiled their attack by leading a charge directly at their calvary horses, breaking their lines, and forcing the Almoravids to flee.

Despite their turbulent history, Rodrigo still acknowledged King Alphonso as his liege lord. When the king was raising an army to protect Toledo's southern borderlands in 1097, Rodrigo sent knights to augment Alphonso's forces—including his own twenty-two-year-old son, Diego—while Rodrigo himself stayed back to protect Valencia.

The fortunes of the son did not match those of the father. Diego was slain by the Almoravids at the Battle of Consuegra. The fight ended in a loss for Alphonso, and dealt a heavy blow to Rodrigo and his wishes for Valencia's succession.

His only son, and heir apparent to Valencia, was now gone. A few years later, Rodrigo's health began deteriorating. His life-force drained after a lifetime of fighting, Rodrigo fell ill and died in Valencia on July 10, 1099, at the age of fifty-six.

Before his death, Rodrigo's two daughters, Maria and Christina, married into the royal courts of Barcelona and Navarre. His wife Jimena stayed in Valencia, ruling as best she could, but after three years of constant harassment by the Almoravid troops, she reached out to her cousin Alphonso for emergency aid. King Alphonso and his forces came, but none of his commanders could defend Valencia as Rodrigo had. Holding this remote coastal kingdom was, they decided, untenable, and Alphonso advised Jimena to abandon the city. The Christians did so in May of 1102, setting Valencia ablaze upon their departure.

So went the life of Rodrigo. Despite a bruising existence, when situations didn't go his way, when the odds were stacked against him, he found a way to turn trials into triumphs. For this trait, even his most vehement Muslim detractor, after first declaring him to be the scourge of his time, then said, "This man—by his unflagging and clear-sighted energy, his virile character, and his heroism—was a miracle among the great miracles of God and his love of glory. Victory always followed the banner of Rodrigo (may God curse him!)."

With Valencia in flames, Rodrigo's body was carried back to Castile. During his lifetime, Rodrigo was forced to earn his bread away from his homeland; only in death was the banished knight able to return. Yet by a stroke of fate, the Campeador's bloodline would one day find its way to Castile's royal throne.

From the last days of al-Mansur to the death of Rodrigo, the eleventh century had been a time when the entire power structure of Spain was remade, but the religious future of Spain still hung in the balance. After taking over Valencia, the Almoravids captured Zaragoza, but then corruption crept into their regime, and internal strife weakened them from within. Soon the

Almoravids incurred several losses to the Christian kings. Eventually the Almohads—a group of North African Berber Muslims—overthrew the Almoravids in both Africa and Spain. They brought reforms to al-Andalus, forbidding the practice of any religion besides Islam, forcing Jews and Christians to choose between conversion, emigration, or death.

Battles raged throughout the twelfth century. Victories came and reverses followed for both Christians and Muslims fighting for supremacy in Spain. Then early in the thirteenth century, a coalition of Christian troops defeated a huge Almohad army and its Caliph al-Nasir at the Battle of Las Navas de Tolosa in 1212 AD.

The Christian forces were led by King Alphonso VIII, the great-great-grandson of the Campeador, Rodrigo Diaz, through the lineage of his daughter, Christina (from a union of the royal families of Castile and Navarre). Alphonso VIII had previously suffered a major defeat at the Battle of Alarcos in 1195, but his resounding victory at Las Navas de Tolosa proved the decisive blow to the Almohads, breaking the Muslim powerhold in Spain and turning the tide for the Christians. And on the eve of that decisive battle, the Campeador's bones were said to have been rattling within their tomb.[71]

After having hung as oil lamps in the Great Mosque of Cordoba for nearly two and a half centuries, Saint James' church bells were finally reclaimed in 1236 by Castile's King Ferdinand III—grandson to Alphonso VIII. Upon conquering Córdoba, he forced Muslim captives to carry the church bells back up to Santiago de Compostela.

While the Islamic influence in Spain was falling, the Christian star was on the rise. Aragon controlled the east of the peninsula, and Portugal the west; Castile became the largest and most powerful, controlling its center.

One day, all the political and religious powers on the peninsula would be ruled by Christian kings and clergy. Spain's national identity took on the spirit of Rodrigo, and songs of his heroism were sung throughout the ages. Rodrigo was named their national hero, and the kings of Spain were his kinfolk.[72] Today, El Cid Campeador Rodrigo Diaz and his wife Doña Jimena Díaz lie in eternal repose under the transept at the center of Burgos Cathedral.

Acceptance

Leaving Burgos today is much more scenic than entering it. First the Camino leads us out of the city's historic district and we're guided through tree-lined streets and garden-filled parks. Soon we're moving along country roads, walking past hay fields and passing through outskirt villages. Along Castile's frontier, sweeping fields take over the landscape, and we're surrounded again by fresh air and open skies.

Traveling the Camino has brought each of us a sense of freedom unlike anywhere else, but no matter the beauty we see, or the history we hear, it's the time walking along the Camino that matters most. With no work, no phones, no "weefee," there's nothing to do but walk, think, reflect, connect, and share.

The hours of walking leave us removed from distraction. Everyone has their own rhythm, their own speed. You might walk with some pilgrims for ten minutes; with others, it may be ten days. When you walk with people for a longer time, you get to know them on a deeper level than you would in normal day-to-day life.

Today the Camino is full of pilgrims both young and old, retirees and drifters, graduates and dropouts, seekers and finders. Anyone and everyone can be found here. While some pilgrims are simply looking to take a break from their traditional lives, others are in search of something different, something *more*.

Many of the older pilgrims are wondering whether or not they've fulfilled their life's purpose, while many of the younger ones are still trying to figure out what that purpose should be, still searching for some spark, some insight on how to proceed, how to live. While life is highlighted by some beautiful moments, it can feel defined by its most trying ones. This proves true as we walk across the Meseta—the central plains of Spain—which finds new ways to toy with our minds and test our resolve.

The Meseta's endless skies are draped over barren landscapes, forming a limitless horizon that we continually travel toward, yet never reach. Walking gravel pathways for days, we cross nothing but open, dusty fields absent of trees, hills, or landmarks of any kind. With nothing by which to gauge progress, it seems as if we're making no forward movement, and time stands still.

While we can see forever in every direction, some villages remain hidden until we're standing right on top of them. Their silhouettes never register on the horizon because they've been built into tiny, pocketed valleys, just out of sight.

When the terrain is both open and flat, we expect to see the town off in the distance as we approach. It's comforting knowing how long we have still to go. So when a town *doesn't* appear up ahead, and there's still no sign of it when we feel we should have already arrived, the mind begins to fret.

Could we have passed the village without seeing it? Was it built off to the side of the road and we somehow missed it?

Is this town even here still? When was this guidebook printed, anyway?

At this point, time returns and the sun begins dropping quickly from the sky. Now you'll start thinking about having to walk to the *next* town, which—just like the last one—is four hours away.

Do I have enough water? Will I get to eat tonight?

The austere emptiness of the Meseta evokes a certain helplessness unfamiliar to many of us living in the civilized world, which can have every convenience outside our door or just a click away. With limited options, all we can do is keep moving forward, keep going further and further into the unknown.

Though we attempt to stay upbeat in the face of the unpleasant prospect of extending the day's journey, the unease remains—until the miraculous moment when that missing village finally reveals itself. And it eventually does, every time, even if it *is* a few kilometers off from what the map had indicated.

Despite some desolate moments, this region can also surprise you with striking landscapes. Large fortresses punctuate grand hilltops. We have a nine-hundred-meter cliff-like slope to zigzag up called Mataburros (the mule-killer). If you'd like a reward for your labor, there are incredible views at the top.

Contrasting with the region's naturally sparse surroundings, huge sandstone churches stand tall over the small pueblos of these flatlands. Up close, the thousand-year-old churches have intricate stone fixtures with revered saints and mythical creatures chiseled onto their walls; however, the haunting winds that barrel through the Meseta have eroded much of their detail, leaving the faces of many of the figures both blank and stark.

The Meseta is considered "grain country," the breadbasket of northern Spain. At this time of year, the wheat and barley fields have already been harvested. The sheep have all migrated south. Besides the surrounding stubble-fields, all that remains are falcons roaming the skies and vultures circling up high, probably waiting for one of us to drop.

Moving along, the clear skies disappear and gray storm-clouds roll in. We begin plodding through incessant rain for five days straight, and I suddenly wish I'd invested in a better rain-coat. Perpetual showers soak right through my poncho and then through any remaining layers. While my waterproof bag keeps the things inside my pack dry, the pack itself still takes on water even with an outer rain-cover, and gets heavier throughout each day's trek.

Parochial albergues welcome pilgrims in, offering us refuge after these many inclement walks. Staying in local convents, everyone dries what we can, then some of us find solace at church during evening prayer. While anticipation for each night's sleep is at an all-time high, eagerness for the next day's walk is in steep decline.

A beady rain begins to fall as we move through heavy mist. Fog restricts the vision to less than a stone's throw in every direction, and I begin to miss the wide-open skies of the Meseta from just a few days ago. Looking up now just gets my eyes peppered with raindrops, so I keep my head down and continue along the puddle-soaked path.

Arriving in Sahagún, we come to one of the older towns along the Camino Francés. Not only was this a thriving Roman center, linking the Seventh Legion back to Rome, but two early Christian martyrs were beheaded here at the beginning of the early fourth century, which led to this place being called Domnos Santos (Holy Lords).

In the eleventh century, Alphonso VI (El Cid's liege lord and king) heavily invested in Sahagún. For the town's support during his war with his brother Sancho, Alphonso granted Sahagún great monastic privileges, giving its Monasterio de San Benito control of nearly a hundred other monasteries across Spain. As a major patron of Santiago de Compostela, Alphonso also annually donated bushels of wheat to Sahagún, feeding thousands of medieval pilgrims on their way to Santiago each year. Sahagún was so dear to the former king that, per his orders, Alphonso was buried here upon his death.

By the twelfth century, this city had been woven into the legends of Charlemagne and Roland. On their fabled quest to liberate the tomb of Saint James in Compostela, Sahagún was listed as the place where Duke Milo, Roland's actual father, was slain by Saracens during the legendary Battle of Sahagún, a tale which spawned the *Miracle of the Flowering Lances*. This legend says that Charlemagne's men stuck their lances into the ground on the eve of battle and, by morning, the lances of the knights who were about to die had grown bark and leafy branches. This was seen as a sign of those knights' impending martyrdom. When those same knights lost their lives fighting, a forest is said to have grown up right where their lances had flowered.

Sahagún is now a modest portrait of its former glory. Today it's a small, weathered, working town that has withstood Spain's turbulent past. While modest in stature, the town is still rich with heritage. Walking around, Sahagún has several grand churches, monasteries, and sanctuaries from the twelfth century. Each displays a mix of architectural styles once prevalent on the peninsula, blending elements of romanesque, gothic, and even mudéjar with Islamic influences. As we leave town, the locals inform us that a grove of poplar trees we pass are the very ones that rose from that fabled battle of Charlemagne and the flowering lances of his knights.

When sifting through the scraps of fact and legend, sometimes it's better to not let reality get in the way of a good story. Other times the truth is more fascinating than the legend itself. The Camino remains full of stories, which keep revealing themselves as we create our own.

Today's history has my undivided attention.
Heavy showers accompanied my walk leaving
Sahagún this afternoon. Upon reaching Calzada
del Coto for the night, my boots are so drenched
that I can enjoy no disillusions of them possibly
drying by morning; and for some reason, this
tiny pueblo doesn't even have one fµ¢king news-
paper for me to crumble up and stuff inside my
boots to help them dry.

If all this water is supposed to be cleansing me
of my sins, I'm probably in need of some more
soaking, but my body's energy is wavering, my
mind's vigor waning. The elements are taking a
toll. The days are adding up. After two more rain-
soaked walks, and with three hundred kilometers still between myself and Santiago, it's time
for another rest day—my third overall—which I
take upon reaching the city of León, on Day 53
of my Camino.

León is a fairly large city, and it takes some
time to walk to its center. Moving from one
barrio to the next, our path guides us to the heart
of the capital of this former kingdom. Colorful

balconies and vibrant storefronts bring its ter-
raced streets to life. Then long corridors lead us
to small plazas with quaint markets, or to grand
ones with classic architecture.

This day of rest serves me well. It gives me
a chance to clean and dry all that I have, while
allowing me time to roam León's lively streets
and arcaded squares. Humbled by a challenging
week crossing the Meseta, it's time to give Mother
Nature her due. She can wear us down. She can
stop us in our tracks. I mustn't be too proud to
recognize when I've reached my limit and stop
and rest to regain strength, because without a
healthy body and strong mind, life's journey
becomes infinitely more challenging.

At dawn I leave León by myself, the yellow
arrows guiding me through the city's historic
streets. There's a calm quietness here at this early
hour, a stark contrast from the revelry I witnessed last night before making my way back to
the albergue at curfew.

The shops and restaurants lining these stone
slab streets are now closed. The outdoor seats of

the cafés are empty and neatly stacked along the
front walls. The crowds of partying Spaniards are
gone, though I'm sure they enjoyed themselves
into the wee hours. My only companions now are
a couple of street sweepers and a few merry bor-
rachos still making their way home.

The yellow arrows guide me by León's grand
cathedral, down a few alleyways, and then out
of the city. Eventually I come to a path traveling
alongside a built-up highway, leading me away
from civilization and back into the obscurity of
the Camino.

It was more than just fatigue weighing on me
in León. Today I walk alone in hopes of resolv-
ing this restlessness. León was the last major city
I'll pass before my eventual arrival to Santiago.
Not only am I getting close to the end of this pilgrimage, I'm approaching the end of this entire
year of travel. In a few weeks' time, I'll be heading
back to the States—without a job, an address, or
any idea of what's to come.

Some angst seems inevitable, but I usually
haven't spent too much time thinking about it.

The end of this trip has always seemed so far away that what lies beyond it hasn't really concerned me. But suddenly, it feels like I'm being shaken from a dream—this dream that, in many ways, came alive once I left my career in DC, a decision that set me on a new path, leaving what was in favor of what could be.

Beyond this journey lies the unknown, yet with big decisions looming—like where to live and what job to take—I must remember that in life, just like on the Camino, we can only see so far ahead. Still we must keep moving forward, because our dreams will die if they go unpursued.

If we know where we want to go, we can always devote time and energy to getting there. The things we dream won't just be given to us— they must be earned, and it's through action, sacrifice, and perseverance that they can be attained. Our paths may be uncertain at times, and—just like in the Meseta—looking too far ahead doesn't always help. What we seek cannot always be seen, but that doesn't mean it's not there.

After doing all I've done and seeing all I've seen, when the time comes, I must be ready to close out this adventure, so I can make room for a new one.

Continuing my life journey, may I view any perceived errors with optimism, using each as an opportunity to learn, so as not to make the same mistake twice.

May I meet every obstacle with enthusiasm, knowing that as each hurdle is overcome, I'll have one less standing in my way.

May I find the courage to push past uncertainty, the strength to withstand pain, and the patience to endure adversity.

Until my dreams become reality, may I have faith that one day, God willing, I'll reach them.

Let me quell this part of me that fears for the future and just be here, now. Now, the only time

I can assess my choices. Now, the only moment I can make decisions. Now, the only instant I can direct my actions.

Moving along, our route brings us through the town of Hospital de Orbigo and we get to walk down its famous medieval bridge. Soon the Camino leads through Astorga, where pilgrims get to see a magical palace by Antoni Gaudí, which now serves as *Museo de los Caminos*, hosting a bevy of religious art dedicated to the Camino. Our path starts to climb once again; the surrounding countryside becomes a scrubland of scattered patches of broom and bramble, accompanied by country roads leading us through slate-roofed medieval villages.

Next our journey leads up into the León Mountains, and that familiar burning sensation returns to our legs. The Camino leaves the paved road and takes us up to high woodlands. Following a leaf-covered trail, our path meanders up the mountainside. We are shaded by silver birch and evergreen trees, and surrounded by scrubs and juniper bushes.

Focusing on the present, I've reconnected with some familiar faces among the pilgrims. Together we weave along the welcoming green slopes of northwestern Spain. Anything concerning the future will have to wait. Our time is full. It's spent rising early to absorb a sunrise in the forgotten village of Foncebadón, venturing off the Camino Francés to catch a sunset above the ancient gold mines of Las Medulas, and staring up at an endless myriad of stars lighting up the sky, some of them racing across the skyline as if chasing one another.

By living in the moment, we find solace in the present. While enjoying life's simple pleasures, we reconnect with our most forgotten faculty—our ability to listen. For in listening to others—whether they speak of their hopes, their dreams, or their struggles—we can understand that we are not alone in our quest for fulfillment. We're all working to make sense of the world, all searching for our place in it.

It's also by tuning in and listening to our inner voice—usually left muffled under deadlines, debts, and excuses—that we can hear the solutions to life's problems. We often find that the answers we seek were there all along, just waiting to be uncovered, forever sounding out of the stillness, stirring up from the silence.

Revelation

Moving down into the El Bierzo valley, the Camino takes us by Ponferada and its magnificent Templar castle, built there back in the thirteenth century to keep watch over the Camino. Traveling through this fertile valley today, we find ourselves walking along undulating hills covered with vineyards and surrounded by mountains in every direction. In a region known for its good food and good wine, the ancient sanctuaries and former hermitages give this place a distinct Old World feel as we walk through one medieval village after another, such as Cacabelos and Villafranca del Bierzo.

Lush rolling ridges accompany us to our left and right as we're led into the narrow Valcarce valley. In the low grounds, we find a unique experience that somehow combines a walk beside rivers, along highways, past hamlets, across parking lots, by cow pastures, through chestnut groves, under motorways, and up country roads all in one eclectic, adventurous afternoon.

Leaving the valley, our path moves up a mountainside dominated by chestnut forests. Under shaded canopies, we travel along tracks covered in dead leaves and fallen nuts, and surrounded by a thick undergrowth of bushes and ferns, home to all kinds of wildlife. A dirt road leads us out of the dense forest and up a high-grassed spur. Our road climbs, moving up the mountainside. Nearing the crest of these highlands, beautiful vistas of green peaks and valleys appear, extending as far as the eyes can see.

We've come to the eastern edge of Galicia, our final region of Spain. The first place we arrive at is O Cebreiro, a small stone village nestled between the Serra do Courel and Serra dos Ancares. Up on this high ridge, cobbled streets weave in and out of the dozen or so existing structures within its confines. Several of them are *pallozas*—circular structures with pointed thatched roofs made of straw and broom, giving this pre-Roman settlement the look of some ancient shire from God knows when.

The houses here are made to withstand the notoriously rough winters in what is now Celtic Spain. Walking around, the streets all lead to one place—La Iglesia de Santa María Real, the oldest church associated with the Camino, a pilgrim's refuge since 836 AD, just two decades after the rediscovery of Saint James' tomb.

The church has thick stone walls and sunken floors to withstand the local snowstorms; the silver structure is capped with a small bell tower. On foggy days, the bells toll to guide pilgrims out of the woods to safety. The church's pink-stone interior has three naves with barrel-vaulted apses. Its central nave has a dozen wooden pews placed to view the high altar, which has a statue of Jesus on the cross. To the right, the lateral nave displays Bibles in dozens of languages, including Braille and Cherokee. Beyond the display case, there's a small chapel dedicated to the events of a particular snowstorm that happened here hundreds of years ago.

At the turn of the fourteenth century, a brutal blizzard began pummeling this mountainside. A peasant farmer named Juan, living in the nearby hamlet of Barxamaior, was determined to attend mass and receive the Eucharist. He fought through the storm's icy snow and turbulent winds to arrive at this church. The priest who was preparing for mass was, as it happened, struggling with his own faith. He was shocked to see Juan, baffled that anyone would have come out in such violent conditions. Considering him a fool, the priest scolded him for risking his life for a bit of bread and wine, but the farmer didn't respond.

The priest carelessly rushed through the mass, but at the moment of consecration, the bread suddenly turned into a pulsing hunk of flesh, and the wine into blood, which then expelled from the chalice to stain the linen-clothed corporal. In awe of what had just transpired, the priest immediately fell to his knees and prayed to God, giving thanks for what he had just witnessed, a miracle simultaneously restoring the faith of the priest while rewarding the devotion of the farmer.

Today the relics of this Eucharistic miracle are displayed in *Capilla del Santo Milagro* (Holy Miracle Chapel). A glass cabinet preserves the chalice, a small plate (paten), as well as the relics. In front of it stands a silver and crystal sacrarium-shrine donated by Queen Isabella and King Ferdinand after a visit during one of their own pilgrimages to Compostela. Lastly, a side wall of this chapel has two stone arches built side by side. Underneath each is a mausoleum—one for the priest, and one for the farmer, both buried here upon their deaths, their two lives forever joined by that fateful mass.

Continuing on, we walk along mountain passes and visit one ancient village after another. We skirt the mountain ridges and peer down over the wooded valleys below. We take in the beautiful views and reflect upon the journey.

Many a life lesson can be extracted from the Camino, a place where the metaphorical realm touches our literal one:

Sometimes, the view behind us is more beautiful than the one in front. Still, this shouldn't distract or deter us from pursuing our goals, which come closer with every step we take.

Holding onto things weighs us down. It's better to figure out what the essentials are, and leave the rest behind.

While journeying with a friend, sometimes we each think the other is paying attention and knows where to go. Then we *both* get lost, because neither one of us was reading the signs.

The Camino certainly looks different today than it did in centuries ago. We now have many comforts unknown to ancient pilgrims, but a pilgrimage can still have as much meaning today as it did back then. Modern pilgrims simply have different challenges to navigate, and misfortune can still find us all.

Today, there's often the desire to take buses or trains forward to avoid physical hardship or unpleasant scenery. Taxi services offer to transport bags forward to a person's daily destination, leaving them to carry only water for the day's journey.

But at what point does a pilgrimage simply become a nature walk? When does the easy way no longer reflect the right one?

Those answers differ for everyone. What is possible for one pilgrim is not always possible for another. Each pilgrim has their own abilities. Each must search their own heart for that answer.

Out here, you get what you put in. If you continually make good use of your abilities, you'll never be left to wonder if you should've done more. Out of all the pilgrims I've met, the most intriguing ones have been those who, despite their physical limitations, found creative ways to move their packs forward.

A Canadian pilgrim with an unwilling back put his bag into a wheelbarrow and pushed it along in front of him.

A Swiss pilgrim with a heart condition hauled his belongings behind him in a wheeled carriage connected by straps to both his waist and shoulders.

Two elderly pilgrims, both of them women, chose to take a bus forward—but only to skip over a particularly steep, rocky downward slope. They knew that if they fell along their descent, there'd be no getting back up.

Then there was an Italian pilgrim with a bum knee that occasionally grew to the size of a grapefruit, yet he walked.

These pilgrims embodied the true meaning of the Camino, revealing the true power of the human spirit.

Heading down the far side of the mountains, we move deeper into Galicia—the land of rivers, meadows, and woodlands—home to the mighty oaks that once built the great Spanish Armada. The path out of the mountains travels into a forested valley beside the Rio Oribio, and the sound of the river's rushing waters soothes us as we make our way across the countryside.

Under cloud-covered skies, our path moves along green rolling hills. Passing mossy walls and ancient hill forts, our walk feels very Celtic. Galicia is certainly a unique part of Spain. It has above-ground cemeteries with niche tombs stacked like cabinets, one atop the other. The hamlets here are all closer together, with only a kilometer or so between them. Even the language here is different. The locals speak Gallego, a regional dialect resembling Portuguese more than Spanish.

The closer we get to Santiago, the more pilgrims appear. Many Caminos have converged from all across Europe, funneling us all to a single point in northwestern Spain. Santiago de Compostela is no longer weeks away, but days now. Our albergues are close to full, even this late in the year.

Traveling along the countryside, we continually pass by cow fields and pig farms. The only buildings out here are farmhouses and the raised grain silos known as *hórreos*. We must be nearing the sea. Restaurants in the towns all offer seafood, serving bowls of mussels and sea scallops, or plates of crab and pulpo (purple octopus pulled in from the Galician shores). For dessert, we enjoy torta de Santiago, an almond crumb cake topped with powdered sugar, or chocolaté con churros—warm strips of fried dough for dipping into a hot cup of creamy chocolate. *¡Delicioso!*

Whether we're ready or not, our arrival to Santiago is now imminent. When we wake up in O Pedrouzo, we're all aware it's officially our last day on pilgrimage. Physically, this flat, short walk is expected to be one of our easiest. Emotionally, it may prove a bit more climactic.

With our bags packed and thrown over our shoulders, the Camino guides us out of town and back into beautiful woodlands. Even in late November, these forests are some of the greenest yet. Not only are the leaves still alive on their high limbs, but many of their trunks are covered with moss and wrapped in ivy.

Winding pathways lead us through primeval forests, and stone markers each kilometer give us a countdown to our final destination.

15 km, 14, 13...

My whole year of travel has come down to this. At this point, on Day 65 of my Camino, I've worn holes into each and every sock I have in my possession. This journey's been so long I can hardly

remember a time that didn't involve waking up
each morning and walking from town to town.

9 km, 8, 7...

Heading up a gradual incline, our route moves
along a quiet residential road. Walking by myself
momentarily, I come to the high point of this
large hill, and there, a mile off in the distance, is
Santiago de Compostela!

From here I can see it only as a collection
of roofs, but it's my first glimpse of the city. It
comes from atop the final hill between me and
my long-pursued goal. The Galicians call this
place *Monte do Gozo*. It means *Mount Joy* in
English, *Mont Joie* in French. The name captures
the feeling I now share with every pilgrim who's
ever stood here before me, or will after.

Finding a few friends, we head down the
street, en route to Santiago's cathedral. Making
our descent, we reach the outskirts of the city. It
seems like we're already beginning the process of
rejoining civilization—we're once again waiting

for streetlights to change, letting cars go by, and looking both ways before crossing.

Life feels like it's not going to be quite the same after this. We've just lived a purer existence from a time forgotten. Each day was marked with meaning, every moment infused with purpose.

On pilgrimage, we're given a chance to observe all that is good in humanity. As pilgrims, we get to be the people we've always aspired to be. Resilient. Generous. Humble. Trusting. Understanding. We get a glimpse of the best version of ourselves, showing that the true treasure lies not only in the fulfillment of our goals. It's the journey itself, and what it teaches us, that's the real gift we each take with us. A pilgrimage will never be about how long you walk or how fast you walk it. What matters most is what you learn along the way.

Following the sidewalk, a two-lane street leads us to the city's center. Walking through the outer and more modern part of Santiago, we pass lines of cars parked in front of white-walled apartment complexes built atop a succession of bancos and supermercados.

The two-lane street eventually turns into one lane. Coming to a busy intersection, we cross the street and pass some small retractable poles sticking out of the ground, acting as a barrier to prevent cars from following us into what's become the older part of town.

We've reached the city's historic district and have just crossed a threshold where, for one last time, we're transported back to a world of centuries past. Surrounded by a city of stone, we walk along corridors with charming balconies hanging over flat-faced storefronts, their glass windows framing the view of the welcoming spaces within.

Cutting through several small plazas, streets come and go in all directions, creating a labyrinth waiting to be explored. Statues of saints or scholars will adorn one plaza, while manicured-bush gardens will beautify the next.

A covered passageway appears at the far side of the following plaza. Approaching, I hear the sound of Galician bagpipes, their vibrations sending joyous ripples of anticipation fluttering through the entirety of my exhausted body.

Stepping through the passageway, we enter a sprawling square. Plaza del Obradoiro is covered by open skies and surrounded by stately buildings. Moving toward its center, we look over our left shoulders, back toward where we came from, and the magnificent beauty of a golden sand-colored cathedral finally comes into view.

The cathedral, covering the entire eastern side of the plaza, captures our attention completely. As we stand at the center of this massive square, our eyes cannot even take in its full breadth. Its robust, fortress-like wings stretch to the adjoining sides of the square, their simple design seeming deliberately chosen to not distract from the imposing, intricate façade that consumes the center, placed between the two baroque bell towers reaching high to the heavens.

The tower on the right side is currently encased in construction materials. It's undergoing renovations and can hardly be seen, but it matters not. This site's significance lives not in the state of these stones, but in the source of their symbolism.

With our Camino now complete, joy fills the air, bags hit the ground, and elation takes over. Our emotions erupt into cheers as we hug and rejoice while processing the concept that we have, indeed, arrived; that this journey is, in fact, over.

We take our time, allowing this sentiment to soak in. We sit down in the square to fully take in the magnificence of the moment. As the excitement begins to subside, the sounds around me seem to fade and I'm overcome by a new feeling— one unlike any I've ever felt. A sense of inexplicable calmness. A soothing serenity that can only be described as peace.

We Catholics have a custom of offering peace to one another during mass, but it is not until this moment that I've truly experienced such a feeling and can really appreciate the gesture. It fills a void within me that no amount of money, accomplishments, possessions, or power ever could. I'm grateful to know that such a state exists—If I ever lose the feeling, at least now I know what to be striving for. Soon enough, I know, this moment will move to memory. We'll each leave the plaza and go on to get our *compostela*, a completion certificate still written in Latin. We'll explore the inside of this ancient cathedral, pay our respects to Saint James, and receive the Church's blessing. Tonight, we'll tour the town and celebrate with whatever energy we can summon before diving into a deep, deep slumber.

For a few days of added reflection, some of us will then continue the journey to the ocean until we reach Finisterre—from the Latin *finis terræ*, meaning 'the end of the world.' Some pilgrims will find their way further north, to the rocks of Muxia, where they'll partake in a tradition of burning a personal possession, saying goodbye to it. Others will simply go there to watch the sun set slowly into the deep blue abyss.

But soon enough, we'll all go our separate ways and begin the journey home—or wherever the next chapter takes us. Completing the Camino doesn't mean that all life's conflicts have been resolved. The end of the Camino is just the beginning. We must continue to go through life, applying what we've learned. Perhaps that's all life really is—learning the lessons put in front of us to figure out how best to live.

In the end, the Camino will mean something different to everyone who walks it. We each must extract our own lessons, find our own meaning to take with us. As the saying here goes, the Camino doesn't give you what you want. It gives you what you *need*. Out here, there is no telling who you will meet, or what you can expect. But no matter where you are called to go, follow the signs and embrace the journey. Life is a gift. When you live it deliberately, there's no telling how it may surprise you.

FIN

CAMINO
PICTURE
GALLERY

You've come this far…now check out
Shawn's photos from his Camino:

SMOKELESSMIRROR.COM/GALLERY

ENJOY THIS BOOK?
HELP MAKE A
HUGE DIFFERENCE

Every successful book has one thing in common, people talk about it. For books, the real power to "get the word out" resides with you, *the reader*. If you enjoyed this book, please spend a few minutes going to your preferred platform to leave a quick review, sharing your thoughts about the book.

THANK YOU. YOUR
SUPPORT IS GREATLY
APPRECIATED!!

ACKNOWLEDGEMENTS

Several good friends were kind enough to read early versions of this story. I owe a great deal of thanks to Daniel Elisii, Margaret McCampbell, Jake Atwell, and Scott Anderson. Their input was essential to the growth of this project. I'm very grateful to my publishing team, including my editor, Elayne Morgan, and her attention to detail; Andy Bridge, and his alluring cover; Nat Case, and his captivating maps; and Colleen Sheehan, and her beautiful interior. Thank you to all of my friends and family for their support over the years. Thank you to everyone I worked with or met at the Doylestown Bookshop.

ENDNOTES

1   Julius Caesar and the Roman Legions fought
to conquer the various Celtic tribes during the
Gallic Wars. Lacking any cohesion, the Gallic
tribes were unable to provide much resistance.
Then Vercingétorix came to power as chief-
tain of the Arverni tribe and united the Gallic
tribes against the Romans. Elected as general
of their unified forces, Vercingétorix led a successful guerrilla warfare campaign against Caesar's army, cutting off their supply chains. In
a pitched fight, he and his confederate army
defeated Julius Caesar and his Roman Legions
at the Battle of Gergovia. The union of the
various Celtic tribes is said to have happened
too late. Caesar's forces regrouped and were
able to withstand further uprisings, which cul-
minated at the Battle of Alesia in 52 BC. When
defeat became imminent, to save the lives of as
many of his people as possible, Vercingétorix
surrendered himself to the Romans. He was
held in captivity for six years until, in 46 BC,
the former king was paraded through the streets
during Caesar's triumph, and then executed by
garrote. Once pacified, the territories of Gaul
would thrive as a Roman province.

2   This area had been inhabited by the Vellavi tribe, a lesser lesser-known tribe than the Arverni, both located in the Auvergne region. The Romans called this city Anicium. The hill itself is Mont Anis.

3   The dolmen on the top of the hill is said to have been venerated for thousands of years before the arrival of the Romans, who built the first temple around it.

4   In the eighth century, an iconoclastic movement coming from the Byzantine east sought to banish idols or remnants from pagan times. Coming to Le Puy, they destroyed the dolmen, all except for a single slab that remains within the church today.

5   King Louis IX stopped in Le Puy in 1245 and 1254 AD while traveling to and from the Holy Land during the Crusades. Upon one of his returns, the king gave this cathedral an ebony image of the Blessed Virgin clothed in a "gold brocade." The king supposedly brought it from the Levant, somewhere in the eastern Mediterranean shores of modern-day Israel, Jordan, Lebanon, and Syria. It was reportedly a gift from the Grand Sultan of Babylon, the ruler of Egypt, and could be a Christianized statue of the mother goddess Isis and her son Horus. In 1794 AD, the original was burned on an execution pyre like a witch during the French Revo-

lution. A replica was made from a sketch drawn by one Faujas de Saint-Fons back in 1777. There are two other stops along the "Le Puy route" that have Black Madonnas. One is at Rocamadour, a variant route taken from Figeac. The other is in Santiago de Compostela, which has a replica of Montserrat's Black Madonna.

6   Pierre Soulage is considered one of the world's greatest living artists. On a visit to Conques at the age of fourteen, he was so moved by what he saw that he decided to devote his life to art. Pierre typically worked with black paint and how light reflects off of it; when he accepted the job of making these church windows, he and master glassmaker Jean-Dominique Fleury created an entirely new glass technique which modulates light in such a way as to allow natural light in while obscuring the view of anyone looking out. Pierre Soulage also has a museum dedicated to his work in Rodez, France (forty kilometers from Conques).

7   It is believed that, at the moment of death, a person's immortal soul will receive judgment as to their destination in the next life; the individual's actions during their lifetime determine where they'll end up. This is considered the Last Judgment, or particular judgment in Christianity. The tympanum at Conques depicts Jesus Christ in the center. Below him is a tipping scale

with Archangel Michael on his right side and
the devil to his left. When the good deeds out-
weigh the bad, the scale tips toward Archangel
Michael and the soul enters the heavenly realms
on Christ's right side, full of joyful people where
everything is pleasant, orderly, and peaceful.
If the scale tips toward evil and the devil, then
the soul goes to the left, where they are met
by all kinds of torments gruesomely depicted
throughout the tympanum's left side. Jesus sits
calmly in the middle presenting a hand to each
side, offering onlookers a choice, which is theirs
to make. This tympanum was meant to educate
an illiterate public, which was the majority at
the time of its creation.

8   Pamela Sheingorn, Book of Sainte Foy (University of Pennsylvania Press, 1996), 288.

9   Thomas Cahill, How the Irish Saved Civilization (Doubleday, 1998), 12.

10   Many discourses have delved into the Messianic prophecy within the Old Testament. For
an extensive study, consider Rydelnik & Blum,
The Moody handbook of Messianic prophecy:
studies and expositions of the Messiah in the
Old Testament (Moody Publishers, 2019).

11   Mathew 7:20-23

12   Mark 3:35

13   1 John 4:7-8

14 Matthew 22:35-40

15 Luke 7:22

16 Matthew 8:27

17 John 1:14

18 Matthew 5:17

19 Gerald Sittser, Resilient Faith: How the Early Christian "Third Way" Changed the World (Brazos Baker, 2019), 22.

20 Sittser, Resilient Faith, 21.

21 Clement of Alexandria, The Instructor 3.6, in ANF 2:280

22 Justin Martyr (100-165 AD), First Apology, ch 67.

23 Sittser, Resilient Faith, 162-163.

24 "On the contrary, they deserve the name of faction who conspire to bring odium on good men and virtuous, who cry out against innocent blood, offering as the justification of their enmity the baseless plea, that they think the Christians the cause of every public disaster, of every affliction with which the people are visited. If the Tiber rises as high as the city walls, if the Nile does not send its waters up over the fields, if the heavens give no rain, if there is an earthquake, if there is famine or pestilence, straightaway the cry is, "Away with the Christians to the lion!" What! shall you give such

multitudes to a single beast? Pray, tell me how many calamities befell the world and particular cities before Tiberius reigned—before the coming, that is, of Christ?"—Tertullian (155-220 AD), Apology XL.

25 Lactantius (250-325 AD), De Mortibus Persecutorum 10.6

26 Eusebius of Caesarea (260-339 AD), Historia Ecclesiastica, Chapter 8

27 Hannah Green, Little Saint (Modern Library, 2001), 14-15.

28 Green, Little Saint, 15.

29 Ibid.

30 Maxentius provoked Constantine to come and fight him. As Constantine and his forces invaded northern Italy, Maxentius left the confines of the Roman capital to engage his rival. They met by the Tiber River next to Milvian Bridge on the northern outskirts of Rome. Constantine's forces were winning the day, and Maxentius and his troops fled, trying to cross the river on a pontoon bridge they had previously built. This bridge broke and many, including Maxentius, drowned in the Tiber during the attempted escape. After the victory, Maxentius' body was fetched out of the river, and his head was cut off and sent to Carthage. After seeing his head, Maxentius' loyalists in Africa relented

and offered their support to Constantine, allowing him to consolidate power over the entire
West.

31 In the Greek-speaking East, Emperor Licinius,
Constantine's one-time ally, began persecut-
ing Christians once again. Constantine fought
and defeated Licinius to become ruler of the
entire empire in 323 AD. Emperor Constantine
founded his capital of Constantinople (modern
day Istanbul) in 330 AD. He ruled the entire
Roman Empire until his death seven years later,
receiving baptism on his deathbed.

32 Sittser, Resilient Faith, 50.

33 Cahill, How the Irish Saved Civilization, 37.

34 Ibid., 27.

35 Sheingorn, Book of Sainte Foy, 13-14.

36 Ibid., 215-218.

37 Green, Little Saint, 11-12.

38 Étape translates loosely to "step" in English, but
it more accurately describes a day's march.

39 La Via Postumia was recently restored, officially
reopening back in 2016. Originally an ancient
Roman road, this pilgrimage route runs across
northern Italy, connecting Genoa to Aquileia.
Historically, it was used by pilgrims heading
to both Jerusalem and Santiago de Compostela. In Norway, St. Olav Ways has also started

to re-emerge. It consists of a network of seven
pilgrim routes—through Norway, Denmark,
and Sweden—all leading to Nidaros Cathedral in Trondheim, where Saint Olav's remains
are buried. The most traveled route is the Gud-
brandsdalen Path, which starts in Oslo. Once in
Trondheim, tradition holds that the pilgrimage
isn't over until a pilgrim walks around Nidaros
Cathedral three times.

40 Acts 12:2

41 Stone cat statues can be found all over La
Romieu. Along the village walls, you'll spot
these felines sitting on stoops, peering over
ledges, peeking out of nooks, and even sneaking
across windowsills. These playful statues were
made by Maurice Serreau and were inspired
by a peculiar legend. Back in 1338 AD, a young
girl named Angeline was living in La Romieu.
Angeline lost her parents when she was young,
but she was adopted by a caring couple nearby.
Not long after, severe weather suddenly caused
a great famine in the village. Due to the lack of
food, cats started going missing as the locals
resorted to eating cat stew. Young Angeline was
appalled to learn of this, so she asked her adop-
tive parents to let her hide several cats in their
attic. Feeling for the girl, they agreed. Angeline hid a male and female cat, who went on
to birth several litters of kittens. When the

weather finally improved, farming flourished once again. But without any cats around, rats began to overrun the town and destroy the village crops. As the villagers fretted to figure out a solution, Angeline announced she now had twenty cats, who would surely help control the rat population. The villagers devised a plan to release the cats all over the village, and the rats soon became a nonissue. In a bizarre twist, as Angeline got older, her appearance began to look more and more feline, with her ears even becoming pointed like a cat's. A bust of Angeline stands in La Romieu today, looking half-woman, half-cat.

42 Einhard & Grant, The Two Lives of Charlemagne, E-book ed. (Digireads, 2010), Kindle, Chapter 9 of The Life of the Emperor Charles written by Einhard.

43 Abd al-Rahman I was a member of the Umayyad Dynasty in Damascus. When the Abbasid Revolution toppled the Umayyad Caliphate (748–750 AD), the twenty-year-old Abd al-Rahman escaped and then survived a perilous journey to Spain. Once there, he won the support of local officials and ascended to power by defeating former governor Yusuf ibn Abd al-Rahman al-Fihri in 756 AD. Abd al-Rahman went on to rule the emirate from its capital city of Cordoba.

44 Sulayman al-Arabi, the pro-Abbasid Wali (gov-
    ernor) of Barcelona and Girona, organized
    a delegation to go to Paderborn in 777 AD,
    requesting military aid from Charlemagne in
    exchange for the submission of the Spanish
    borderlands, including the allegiance of Abu
    Taur of Huesca and Husayn of Zaragoza. After
    intense conflict during the Umayyad invasion
    of Gaul between 719-759 AD, Charlemagne was
    open to pursuing this counter-alliance with
    the Abbasid Empire. He was also given assur-
    ance that the caliph of Baghdad, Muhammad
    al-Mahdi, would be sending forces to Spain to
    subdue the Umayyad powerbase in Cordoba.

45 In 778, Charlemagne gathered all the troops
    he could, and they marched into Spain. When
    they arrived at Zaragoza, they were welcomed
    by Sulayman al-Arabi and his troops, but the
    Wali, Husayn of Zaragoza, would not open the
    city doors, saying he had never promised Char-
    lemagne his allegiance. Husayn had supposedly
    been emboldened by a victory over an Umayyad
    general, Thalaba ibn Obeid, in a recent battle,
    and he no longer felt he needed the alliance.

46 While Charlemagne ordered a siege of the city,
    he did not have his siege engines. Sometime
    during the month-long siege, the invasive force
    sent by the Baghdad caliphate was supposedly

stopped near Barcelona, further isolating Charlemagne on the Iberian peninsula.

47 Charlemagne began to distrust Sulayman
    al-Arabi after he was denied entry into Zara-
    goza; he eventually had him arrested. This trig-
    gered al-Arabi's sons, Matruh and Ayshun,
    to devise a plan to free their father. Arab
    source ibn al-Athir states that once Charlem-
    agne felt completely safe away from Muslim
    lands, al-Arabi's sons and their troops attacked,
    freeing their father and then returning to Zara-
    goza with him. Surviving sources do not say the
    exact location of the attack, only that it was suc-
    cessful and al-Arabi was freed. Ramón Menén-
    dez Pidal, La Chanson de Roland et la tradition
    épique des Francs (Editions A. et J. Picard et
    Cie, 1960) Chapitre VI: L'événement Historique.

48 The Latin annals from the Carolingians only
    credit the Basques for the attack at Roncevaux
    Pass, so later critique of the legend has mostly
    removed the Saracen role from the attack. His-
    torians have claimed that the Arab source could
    have described a separate attack, even though
    both the Latin and Arab annals describe an
    attack when Charlemagne felt he was safely
    away from Muslim lands, and one launched on
    the rearguard, which is where prisoners and
    luggage like gold were held in military forma-
    tions. With Charlemagne's pristine military rep-

utation, it is highly unlikely that his rearguard
would have been defeated twice on their departure from Spain. What is likely is that Christian
officials would have downplayed the Muslim
role in the attack (Charlemagne's only military
defeat) while the Arabs would have highlighted
their own role in the battle. Ramón Menéndez Pidal, La Chanson de Roland et la tradition
épique des Francs (Editions A. et J. Picard et
Cie, 1960) Chapitre VI: L'événement Historique.

Although Sulayman al-Arabi was freed and
Husayn of Zaragoza maintained control of his
city, things still didn't pan out well for either
one. Sulayman al-Arabi was killed by Husayn of
Zaragoza in 780 AD. Abd al-Rahman I subdued
Zaragoza around that same time, and Husayn
of Zaragoza was killed shortly after.

49 Léon Gautier, Chivalry, Tumblar House, 2015,
E-book ed. Chapter II—The Code of Chivalry.

50 Dante, The Divine Comedy, Paradiso, Canto 18.
43-45.

51 This legendary tribute of virgins (fifty nobles
and fifty commoners) is typically associated
with the reign of Mauregatus (783–789). While
many Christian men and women were enslaved
by Muslim forces, and some Christian women
were legitimately married to Muslim men, this
legend has only been traced to chronicles found
after the forged Privilegio del voto, written

around 1150. The voto describes the legendary Battle of Clavijo.

52 Web article by AMDG: "The Legend of Santiago Matamoros (Saint James the Moorslayer)", 25 Jul. 2009,
    http://layijadeneurabia.com/2009/07/25/the-legend-of-santiago-matamoros-saint-james-the-moorslayer/

53 In Muslim Spain, Jews and Christians were treated as second-class citizens. Before that, the Jews were mistreated by the Christians of Spain during the Visigoths' rule. Christians later became upset with the Jews in Spain because the Spanish Jews helped the North African Muslims conquer the peninsula. The Jews kept Christian resistance at bay long enough for the North African Muslims to populate and subdue the country, a fact that the Spanish Christians never forgot. Kirstin Downey, Isabella: The Warrior Queen, (Anchor Books, 2015), 9-22.

54 Richard Fletcher, The Quest for El Cid, (Hutchinson, 1989), 16.

55 The most valuable spoils were the beautiful girls, preferably blond- or red-haired ones from Galicia, Navarre, and Francia, who were described as having blue eyes, large breasts, wide hips, thick legs, and perfect teeth. Belén Holgado Cristeto. Tras las huellas de las mujeres

christianas de al-Ándalus. In Actas del Con-
greso Conocer al-Andalus, perspectivas desde el
siglo XXI. Edición de Maria Mercedes Delgado
Perez & Gracia López Anguita. (Ediciones Alfar,
2010), 111. "la predilección que tenian por las
rubias y pelirrojas gallagas, vasconas y francas."
Mercedes Arriaga Flórez, Rodrigo Browne
Sartori, José Manuel Estévez Saá y Victor Silva
Echeto. Sin Carne: representaciones y simula-
cros del cuerpo feminino: tecnología, comuni-
cación y poder.(Arcibel Editores, 2006), 342.

56 Ramón Menéndez Pidal, The Cid and His Spain,
translated by Harold Sutherland, (Routledge
Library Editions: Muslim Spain, 2016), E-book
ed., Chapter II—Spain from Almanzor to the
Cid.

57 Pidal, The Cid and his Spain, Chapter II—Spain
from Almanzor to The Cid.

58 With Sancho dead, their youngest brother
Garcia decided to leave exile in Seville to
go reclaim his throne in Galicia. Thinking
Alphonso and Urraca were his allies, Garcia
accepted an invitation from his brother and
sister to meet in León. Upon his arrival,
however, Alphonso's troops seized Garcia and
locked him in chains. While Sancho had been
content to let his brother live out his days in
exile, Alphonso took no such chance. Garcia
remained captive in the castle of Luna near

León, and although he was treated with royal honors, he remained shackled there until his death seventeen years later.

59 From Historia Roderici, Chapter 14-16, translated and annotated by Simon Barton and Richard Fletcher, The World of El Cid: Chronicles of the Spanish Reconquista, (Manchester University Press, 2000), 106-107.

60 From Historia Roderici, Chapter 22-23, Barton & Fletcher, The World of El Cid, 110-112.

61 Al-Kadir was so despised in Toledo that he had to pay King Alphonso for protection. He put the cost of Alphonso's protection on his own people, which made him even more unpopular.

62 An important development from Alphonso's conquest was that Toledo's Arab libraries were not pillaged. Instead, a translation center was established in which books in Arabic and Hebrew were translated into Castilian, and then from Castilian into Latin, allowing the long-lost ancient knowledge of math, science, and medicine to once again spread throughout Western Europe.

63 Pidal, The Cid and his Spain, E-book ed., Chapter VIII: The Exile and the Emperor—The Cid Eclipsed by the Emperor.

64 Pidal, The Cid and his Spain, E-book ed., Chapter IX: The Revival of Islam—2. Yusuf, Emir of the Faithful.

65 From Historia Roderici, Chapter 35. In Barton & Fletcher, The World of El Cid, 118-121.

66 In Islam, a fatwa is a formal ruling by a theological scholar on a point on Islamic law.

67 From Historia Roderici, Chapter 57. In Barton & Fletcher, The World of El Cid, 136.

68 Pidal, The Cid and his Spain, E-book ed., Chapter XIII: The Cid Subdues the Rebel City— 2. Surrender of the Besieged: The Cid's Speech on the Government of the City.

69 Pidal, The Cid and his Spain, E-book ed., Chapter XIII: The Cid Subdues the Rebel City— 2. Surrender of the Besieged.

70 Some Valencians considered a life lived under a Christian banner an unfit one, and chose to leave. Though he granted them safe conduct for their journey, Rodrigo would not allow them to take their wealth with them.

71 Pidal, The Cid and his Spain, E-book ed., Chapter XVII: The Hero—3. Exemplariness.

72 The Poem of El Cid writes it as, "Behold the honour that cometh to him that was born in lucky hour! Today the kings of Spain are his kinsfolk."

THANK YOU, GOD, FOR GIVING
ME THE OPPORTUNITY TO NOT
ONLY WALK THE CAMINO, BUT TO
TAKE PART IN THIS WONDERFUL
JOURNEY CALLED LIFE.
I AM TRULY BLESSED!

CPSIA information can be obtained
at www.ICGtesting.com
Printed in the USA
LVHW111600171122
733426LV00024B/558/J

9 798985 779905